Amelia Boynton ROBINSON

Matriarch of the Voting Rights Movement

A BIOGRAPHY BY RONNIE BARNES

This book is a work of nonfiction. Names, characters, places, and incidents either are products of the author's research of real and true events or some names may be imaginary names or are used fictitiously to protect the identity of the person involved. Any resemblance to actual persons, living or dead, events, or locales are true to its entirety and not coincidental.

Legal Disclaimer: This book is based, in part, upon actual events, persons, voting and civil rights organizations

ISBN: 978-173-54442-0-8

Cover photo: Leon Frazier

Cover design: David James

Ronnie K. Barnes: visit my website at RonnieTheWriterBarnes.com

Printed in the United States of America First Printing: August 2020

VOTE

A vote-less people is a hopeless people

—Amelia Boynton Robinson

There is no Negro problem, there is only an American problem, and we meet here tonight as Americans... to solve that problem.... It is not just Negroes, but really, it's all of us who must overcome the crippling legacy of bigotry and injustice. And—we—shall—overcome.

—PRESIDENT LYNDON JOHNSON

I dedicate this book to the family of Amelia Boynton Robinson, "The Matriarch of the Voting Rights Movement."

Thank you for allowing me to be a part of sharing the legacy of this special iconic great heroine who changed the lives of everyone in this country and beyond. She is known by some as "The Mother of the Voting Rights Movement." Thank you, "Queen Mother" for giving us the right to vote. And finally, thank you for teaching us how to love humanity.

—Ronnie Barnes

NOTE TO THE READER

This book includes slang language that was used at the time of the civil rights movement through the present day. Some, like "Black" and "White" continue to be acceptable, while other words such as "nigger," "colored," and "Negro" are now considered to be offensive. These terms, especially "nigger," are meant to degrade African Americans—both then and now. They are included for historical reference in order to help the reader understand that era and are not in any way intended to harm, degrade or offend anyone.

SELMA TO MONTGOMERY MARCH

(Google Images)

CONTENTS

PREFACE

I started working on this biography in the fall of 2018. I had completed a book in the spring of 2018 and began to think about something else that would keep my interest and be of importance to me and perhaps something that would fascinate the world.

My first thought was to write about spiritual beings having a human experience. But as I pondered these things, while washing my face and watching my reactions in my bathroom mirror, I thought I'd heard and recognized an inner voice from the spirit of an ancestor saying, "I want you to write my biography." Sounds crazy, huh?!

Well, guess what? I heard that same voice twice, but I thought maybe it was just my imagination running away with me. I chuckled and thought to myself, *No it isn't.*

I tested my theory one more time by essentially saying to the ancestor, "If you want me to write your biography, let me hear you say it one more time." And the spirits of our ancestors spoke once again and said, "Yes."

I had just finished a writing class, which had taught me how to write biographies along with other genres. So, I figured what better time than now to answer the call from my ancestors. I wondered if the whisper I felt talking to me might be "Queen Mother" Amelia Boynton Robinson.

I had met her in person in 2014 during a black history program that I had narrated at my place of employment. She looked great dressed in gold and black attire, which were coordinated with her gold earrings.

As our guest speaker that day, Miss Boynton Robinson spoke distinctly about the progress we had made with voting and civil rights since the 1960s. But she also noted that we still had a ways to go. At the unofficially documented age of around 108 years-old, Boynton Robinson spoke to the audience and said, "I see my work is not done yet."

Incredible, I thought. I was honored and impressed and felt proud to have the "Mother of the Voting Rights Movement" sitting right there in a federal government office speaking to me and my co-workers about the history of voting and civil rights and was encouraging the next generation. In fact, she said in her speech, as she smiled with excitement, "If my mother were here today, she would be so proud of the progress we've made and how far we've come."

FOREWORD

The civil rights movement in Selma, the seat of Dallas County, Alabama has deep roots in the heart of the "Black belt" of the United States. From 1865 to 1875, the Thirteenth Amendment to the Constitution and the Reconstruction across Alabama brought a degree of freedom to the lives of African Americans in southern states that was not always welcome. One uncertainty was the question of the federal government's commitment to enforce its own laws in the South concerning Whites respecting the newly emancipated African American citizens.

With little support from the Union states, White-on-Black violence increased because of the changing of role of Negroes from being slaves to now having full citizenship and freedom. Although the Freemen's Bureau was put into place to oversee the transition of Blacks from slavery to freedom, the federal government did little to encourage Whites to accept this new civil rights freedom of Negroes. So, by the turn of the century, a new racial system had been put in place in the South to disenfranchise Black voters and contaminate the system with racial segregation.

President Andrew Johnson took over after President Lincoln's assignation and his administration would ratify the Thirteenth Amendment, which outlawed slavery. His plan did not provide much protection for the newly freed slaves and ultimately would allow Jim Crow Laws and "Black Code Laws" to require African Americans to sign yearly labor contracts. And, in other ways it limited the Freedmen's economic options and restored plantations back over to White land owners.

It wasn't until the early 1930s that a racist, discriminatory and segregated southern county found Samuel and Amelia Boynton making their mark on Selma, Alabama—something that would change the course of that city and Dallas County, and which, in retrospect, would transform the path of the world .

The Boyntons first impact on Selma could be seen when they taught Black people how to deprogram themselves from what the White supremacy leaders had told them. They reminded Blacks who they were, and this would be the first step in enlightening the Negro mind to feel that he was truly emancipated and entitled to full citizenship in America. Blacks in Selma and the rural counties needed to be taught how to maneuver around being controlled by Jim Crow laws. Yes! Samuel and Amelia Boynton would be that change for Selma. The Boyntons would both make history as well as change the course of the history of the United States of America by ultimately playing a key role in giving Blacks the right to vote, for example, by inviting the Reverend Dr. Martin Luther King Jr. to Selma. Their perseverance and influence would play a major role in initiating the march from Selma to Montgomery, Alabama.

PROLOGUE

Today, many continue to ask the same questions that were asked in previous decades. Does the United States still remain nowhere close to racial parity? The answer is that, in some ways, "Yes, it is" and in other ways "No, it is not."

Let's consider 2016, when the United States celebrated its 240th birthday. It goes back even before Thomas Jefferson and the other founders declared independence. Americans were engaged in a polarizing debate over racial disparities such as why they exist and persist, and over why White Americans as a group were prospering more than Black Americans as a group.[1]

Amelia Boynton Robinson, Matriarch of the Voting Rights Movement recounts the history of why she is "The Matriarch" and to some the "Mother of the Voting Rights Movement." Amelia Boynton Robinson was not only a civil rights leader who pioneered and championed voting rights for African Americans, but in many ways she became a modern-day Harriet Tubman.

She was viciously beaten for helping to lead a 1965 civil rights march that drew national attention to the civil rights movement and which became known as "Bloody Sunday." She was also the first black woman to run for Congress in Alabama.

America's first-century, racist theological ideas are viewed as critical in

---

[1] Ibram X. Kendi, Stamped From The Beginning: The Definitive History of Racist Ideas in America (Bold Type Books, 2016), 3.

sanctioning the growth of American slavery and allowed it to get a pass in Christian churches. History documents that the ideas headlined in the sermons of America's early well-known preachers and intellectuals like Puritans Cotton Mather, John Cotton and Richard Mather, helped bring fifteenth-century racist ideas to America from Europe.

To authenticate American slavery and win converts, Cotton Mather preached racial inequality "in body" while insisting that the dark souls of enslaved Africans would become White when they became Christians.[2] Theories of scientific revolution would be used to justify Mather's writings and sermons which were widely read in the colonies and in Europe to argue that Africans were brought to those regions as part of racial progress. Later, Jim Crow laws would lead to the racist policies of the late nineteenth century. The outlawing of Jim Crow in 1964 passed on racial progress, but it would be the legalization of disguised and unplanned discrimination that brought about more racist policies in the late twentieth century.

So, you may ask, "How does this all tie into the life and times of Amelia Boynton Robinson, The Matriarch of the Voting Rights Movement?" She was a woman of many historical firsts and played a pivotal role in the civil rights movement. Her determination and persistent work even inspired Dr. Martin Luther King Jr. to join the Selma-to-Montgomery march in Alabama.

Although the Civil Rights Act of 1964 forbade discrimination in voting on the basis of race, efforts by civil rights organizations such as the Southern Christian Leadership and the Student Nonviolent Coordination

---

[2] Ibid., 6-7.

Committee pushed the issues to register Black voters who were continuously met with brutal resistance in southern states such as Alabama, Mississippi, Louisiana and Georgia when it came to the right to vote.

I relentlessly tried to figure out why America, and in particular the southern states, fought for Jim Crow laws and the refusal to give African Americans full citizenship in the United states. My first thoughts were to look back over the past 400 years when the first blacks crossed the Atlantic Ocean from west Africa on slave ships, landing in Jamestown, Virginia.

Should I start there or just fast forward to the Reconstruction period? I decided the latter would be a good place to start. According to Dr. Claude Anderson, the founding father and former president of PowerNomics of America Incorporated and the Harvest Institute Incorporated, a reconstruction period was put into place to reconstruct Black people to fit into American society. By definition, the Reconstruction era extended from 1863 to 1877. This would mark a significant chapter in the history of American civil rights.

As we know, the Union victory in the Civil War 1865 may have given some 4 million slaves their freedom, but the process of rebuilding the South during Reconstruction introduced a new set of challenges between 1865 and 1877.[3]

President Andrew Johnson's administration passed new southern state legislation in 1865, and in 1866 restricting "black codes" were enacted to control the labor, behavior and rights of former slaves. He feared it would

---

[3] "History." Selma to Montgomery March. (2019): https://www.history.com/topics/black-history/selma-montgomery-march#section_1.

drive the border states loyal to the Union into the Confederacy and in retrospect anger more conservative northers.

President Johnson's Radical Reconstruction began in 1867 which led to the victory of giving enfranchised blacks a voice in government for the first time in American history. This allowed blacks to win election seats in southern state legislatures and even in the U. S. Congress.

This new-found freedom with full civil rights and legal rights to vote ended in less than a decade because malicious hate groups, including the Ku Klux Klan, rose up and tried to manipulate and reverse the changes of Radical Reconstruction. This resulted in violent a backlash that ultimately restored white supremacy in the South.

With the outbreak of the Civil War, President Abraham Lincoln chose not to make abolition of slavery a goal of the Union war effort. This angered radical abolitionists in the North.

On the contrary, if we revisit when President Lincoln did not have a choice but to stand up for the rights of blacks because slaves were protesting to Union soldiers as they marched through the northern States of the confederacy states. This led to Lincoln being convinced that emancipation had become both a political and military necessity.

Lincoln responded by giving his Emancipation Proclamation—a event that freed more than three million slaves in the Confederate states by January 1, 1863. The Emancipation Proclamation also opened the door for Blacks to enlist in the Union Army, reaching at total of 180,000 Black Union soldiers by the end of the war. On April 11, 1865 Lincoln proposed that some Blacks, including free blacks and those enlisted in the military, deserved the right to vote. Because of his stance for racial equality, he was assassinated three days later and the right for Blacks to vote would fall to his successor as plans for reconstruction were put in place.

At the end of May 1865, President Andrew Johnson presented plans for reconstruction and to uphold the abolition of slavery in compliance with the Thirteenth Amendment to the Constitution. In early 1866, Congress passed the Freedmen's Bureau and Civil Rights Bill specifically for the benefit of Blacks. These new laws would give Negroes who were born in the United States full citizenship and enjoy equality before the law. But Johnson vetoed the bills, causing a permanent rift in his relationship with Congress that ultimately would end in his impeachment. In 1868, the Civil Rights Act became the first major bill to become law over presidential veto.[4]

In February 1869, Congress approved the Fifteenth Amendment and adopted it in 1870 which guaranteed that a citizen's right to vote would not be denied on the account of race, color, or previous conditions of enslavement.

Nonetheless, the struggle to deal with the eradication of slavery continued for another one hundred years with laws being put in place under Jim Crow that would continue in the South and elsewhere until reconstruction would be revived during the civil rights movement of the 1960s—as African Americans fought for the political, economic and social equality that they had been denied continually. A look at the history of the South before the 1960s points shows that blacks were beginning to get bold enough and smart enough to stand up for their rights against Jim Crow

---

[4] Ibid., 3-5.

laws. Samuel William "Bill "and Amelia Platts Boynton who would be a part of that new South where they initially laid the groundwork for what was coming next in the not-so-distant future.

It was in the 1930s, as President of Registration and Voting for the Fourth Congressional District, that Samuel and his wife Amelia revived the Dallas County Voters League as well as laid the foundation for the Voting Rights Act. After Samuel died in 1963, Amelia kept her promise to him that she would continue to fight for voting rights for Blacks. Boynton Robinson became one of the faces of this battle on that cold wintery day while marching in Selma on March 7, 1965, known today as "Bloody Sunday"—a day that eventually led to the Voting Rights Act becoming law in 1965.

Sam and Amelia Boynton's early activism included holding African American voter registration drives in Selma, Alabama from the 1930s through the mid-1960s.

The Reverend Dr. Martin Luther King Jr. would join Southern Christian Leadership Conference and the Student Nonviolent Coordinating Committee along with Amelia Boynton and other civil rights leaders to develop what would become a worldwide human rights movement. Studies have shown that the victories in Eastern Europe, Southern Africa and China all bear the influence of the Selma movement.

Boynton Robinson is best recalled in American history as one of two women who were beaten unconscious and left to die on the Edmund Pettus Bridge in Selma, Alabama. The other woman was Marie Foster who stood behind the six men at the front of the march who were gassed.

A photo of a bloodied Amelia Boynton appeared on the front page of newspapers across the country, drawing attention to the cause of voter discrimination and the violence perpetrated against African Americans. Mrs. Boynton would participate in two subsequent marches, including the protest march to Montgomery on March 24, 1965 along with over 25,000 other protesters. By March of the following year, the number of registered voters in Selma and the surrounding counties had grown from 300 to an estimate 11,000.

Years later, Amelia Boynton Robinson served as vice chair of the Schiller Institute where she promoted civil and human rights. She continued to tour and speak in the United States and internationally on behalf of the Schiller Institute, which she describes its mission as "working around the world to defend the rights of all humanity to progress—material, moral and intellectual until 2009."

In 1990, Boynton Robinson's achievements resulted in her being awarded the Martin Luther King Jr. Medal of Freedom. In 2014, a new generation learned about Boynton Robinson's contributions to the civil rights movement with the premiere of the Oscar-nominated film *Selma*—a historical drama about the 1965 voting rights marches. The world would see Lorraine Toussaint portray Boynton Robinson in the film. And in 2015 Boynton Robinson, at the documented age of 109, marched with President Barack Obama and fellow civil rights activists across the Edmund Pettus Bridge to commemorate the 50th anniversary of the Selma-to-Montgomery March. In August of the same year, Amelia Boynton Robinson would pass away at the age of 110.

"A vote-less people is a hopeless people." Boynton Robinson said—and it was her husband Samuel Boynton's motto. A sign displayed in the window outside the Boyntons' business on Franklin Street also displayed the slogan. In fact, before any business conversations were held with the Boyntons at the office, the first question a visitor would be asked concerned voting. "Are you a registered voter?" If the answer was no, Sam would ask, "Why not?" Amelia Boynton Robinson gave hope a voice and eminently she presented to African American people throughout the South and across the country the right to vote.

Today, African American voting rights have come under scrutiny once again. This time, it's because of voting disenfranchisement. Gutting the vote, voter suppression, voter ID laws, gerrymandering, voter purging, and "Jim Crow 2.0" are all campaigns to frustrate people out of their basic right, according to what Carol Anderson, the author of *One Person, No Vote* lays out in her book. Since 2015, states have been attempting to bring voter registration into the twenty-first century with automatic voter registration program and modernization in the states. This will include electronic registration at DMVs, online registration, election day registration, portability, and pre-registration. Many states across the country are successfully using components of voter registration modernization.[5] The Voting Rights Act has been among the most successful pieces of federal legislation in the history of the country. However, in 1913, the Supreme Court case Shelby County v. Holder struck down the coverage formula that determined which jurisdiction had to "preclear" changes to their election rules with the federal government before implementing them, based on their history of race-based voter discrimination.

The U. S. Court of Appeals for the Fourth Circuit stuck down the law in July 2016, finding that it targeted "African Americans with almost

[5] Newkirk II, Vann R. "The Democrats' New Voting-Rights Moment." The Atlantic, March 2, 2019.

surgical precision." The court ruled that HB 589 violated Section 2 of the Voting Rights Act of the Constitution.[6]

The Voting Rights Advancement Act, initially introduced in the House by Representative Terri Sewell of Alabama and in the Senate by Patrick Leahy of Vermont, sought to restore and extend key provisions of the Voting Rights Act that had been neutralized.[7] The VRRA bill was introduced twice by Sewell in 2015 and 2017, and in 2019, a third version failed to pass with a majority vote in the Senate.

---

[6] Anderson, Carol. "One Person, No Vote: How Voter Suppression Is Destroying Our Democracy." Bloomsbury Publishing Inc. Bloomsbury Publishing, 2018.
[7] Newkirk II, Vann R. "The Democrats' New Voting-Rights Moment." The Atlantic, March 2, 2019.

A Letter to Amelia Boynton Robinson from Marius J. "Ace" Anderson

A letter was given to me from civil rights leader Marius J. "Ace" Anderson that shows a vivid sense of the horrors and injustices that we encountered in this struggle to win our rights as full American citizens:

> I was with you the night of horror in Marion. It was you and I who concealed Reverend C.T. Vivian from a white mob threatening to kill him. Do you remember me breaking through a human barrier at the entrance of the Pettus Bridge by ambulance to evacuate you and others, the day of Bloody Sunday. Do you remember me picking up Reverend James Reeb off the street the night of his slaying? He was carried to Burwell infirmary and later transferred to University Hospital, Birmingham. I, along with Dr. Dinkins and Charles Williams, met with much hostility getting to Birmingham. I made the call also to pick up Viola Liuzzo, but I was told very hostilely that nothing had happened, and the State Troopers gave me an ultimatum of three minutes to evacuate the area. She was later picked up by a white funeral director of Montgomery. Yet I could see her bowed down over the steering wheel of her car flooded with blood. One of the doors was open, and that allowed the courtesy lights in the car to remain on, in spite of the loss of control after the contact of the bullet."
>
> —Marius J. "Ace" Anderson

Note: Ace Anderson was a D. J. in Selma, AL on WTQX radio station from the 60s to the 80s. He also worked at radio station WARMAN-Montgomery, Alabama, 1950-1959.

CHAPTER 1
AMELIA'S EARLY LIFE

I was brought up by people who loved others. I love people. We had no animosity. We had no feeling that we hate anyone.

—AMELIA BOYNTON ROBINSON

Amelia Isadora Platts Boynton Robinson was thought to be born in 1911 and was reared in Savannah, Georgia. But contrary to that documented date of birth, Henry "Hank" Sanders (who was a Democratic member of the Alabama Senate who represented the 23rd District) discovered her true date of birth: "I saw her driver's license when I visited her just three days before she passed. It read '1905,'"[8] Senator Sanders confirmed. He added that she was 110 years old, although most records document Amelia Boynton Robinson to be 104 years old when she died. Boynton Robinson had noted and stated for the records that her true birthday was August 18, 1905.

So, let us start here with Amelia's early life and her upbringing as a child.

[8] Hank Sanders, "Amelia Boynton shook the world, leaves a giant legacy. https://www.al.com/opinion/2015/08/amelia_boynton_shook_the_world.html

Like most African American families both then and now, the Platts family carried a mixture of African, Native American, and German features on both parents' sides. Boynton Robinson grew up in a two-story wooden house in Savannah, Georgia where her father owned a wholesale wood lot. "The principle of doing unto others as you would have them do unto you," as defined in Scripture (Luke 6:31, King James Version), made an impression on young Platts, preparing her for whatever the future might hold.

Her parents had ten children, and Boynton Robinson took pride in acknowledging the contributions of her siblings to society. In *Bridge Across Jordan,* Amelia notes that her parents, George Platts and Anna Eliza Hicks Platts, pushed them to strive to be an example for others and never to hate, but rather to turn hate into love.[9]

Early in the twentieth century, Amelia Boynton's family would make great contributions to America. "I was very proud of every member of our family," Robinson had said.[10] Again, in *Bridge Across Jordan,* the following businesses and professions of members of her family stood out: chairmen, teachers, executive board members, military personnel, singers, dentists, doctors, professional athletes, attorneys, federal employees, poets, and authors/lectures. Maybe it could be said that had not the courageous Amelia Platts Boynton Robinson gone to Selma, Alabama and became the home demonstration agent (teaching home economics) in Dallas County after graduating from Tuskegee Institute, possibly there wouldn't been a

---

[9] Boynton Robinson, Amelia P. and Schiller Institute. *Bridge Across Jordan*. (Washington, D. C.: Schiller Institute, 1991), 12.
[10] Ibid., 4.

civil rights march known today as "Bloody Sunday." Is that too farfetched to contemplate? This question remains debated among scholars to this day.

Amelia's introduction to politics began at an early age: "I can clearly remember going about with Mother in her horse and buggy in the city of Savannah in 1921, when I was ten years old. My induction into politics was knocking on doors and ringing doorbells, giving women the proper information, taking them to the registration board and or taking them to the polls to cast their votes."[11] Family was very important and valued by Amelia, who would often say that if she were to die and could come back to this earth with choice as to family: the same parents, siblings and community would be chosen because of the value and impression of life and character her parents had instilled in them as children.

According to Robinson's journals while growing up in the south, their house stayed crowded with children from the community. Her parents took pride in encouraging the neighborhood children to attend school. The Platts' home was open as a shelter for adults who had been evicted with nowhere else to go.

It was not by chance that Amelia felt it was her destiny to recite a poem during a program at the A.M.E. church in Savannah. In her journal, Amelia recalls the poem "Melinda Sings," by Paul Lawrence Dunbar. Not realizing that she had made an impression in her recitation or singing, Robinson recalls being surprised when a couple wanted to see her.

Amelia noted in her diary that the couple's name was Mr. and Mrs. E.J.

---

[11]Ibid., 11.

Bruce. They were an elderly couple living in Savannah and most importantly, both had been former instructors at Tuskegee Institute. Amelia journaled where she visited the Bruces' home on several occasions because she was interested in a small room with memorabilia related to Dr. Booker T. Washington, Dr. George Washington Carver, Tuskegee Institute, and other key people connected with the establishment of the school. This impressed young Amelia so much that this was the college she chose to attend. Among his credits, Dr. Booker T. Washington is the founding father of Tuskegee Institute—a school that has been a vital institution in the history of African Americans, as Amelia notes.

Amelia vividly spoke about Dr. George Washington Carver in her *Bridge Across Jordan* as someone with whom she became dear friends while a student at Tuskegee Institute: Dr. George Washington Carver could never be appreciated fully unless someone were given the opportunity to know him personally. Students would walk and talk with him and feel some hope for the world through his closeness of communication with God—something Amelia pointed out in the aforementioned book. Dr. Carver meant more to Amelia and her family than anyone would ever know, she said. As a home economics major at Tuskegee, she recalls Dr. Carver being a guest instructor at least four times during her senior year.

CHAPTER 2
AMELIA PLATTS

Only until all human beings begin to recognize themselves as human beings will prejudice be gone forever. People ask me what race I am, but there is no such thing as race. I just answer: "I'm a member of the human race."

—AMELIA BOYNTON ROBINSON

Young Amelia graduated from Tuskegee Institute and moved back to Savannah, Georgia where she worked for about a year as a teacher in the Rosenwald school system in St Mary's, Georgia. The school was located on the St. Mary's River across the river from Fernandine, Florida. She taught there for about a year before being dismissed by the principal for voicing her opinion on a particular matter. At her mother's suggestion, she moved back to back to Philadelphia where her parents lived.

After about a year in Pennsylvania, she returned to Georgia where she taught home economics at a Baptist boarding school in Americus. From there, Amelia accepted a job with the U.S. The Agriculture Department (which was located in Selma, Alabama) and she became the home demonstration agent for Dallas County. She would make Selma her home for the next 50 years.

Upon arriving in Selma in 1930, Amelia met Samuel William ("Bill") Boynton who was the county extension agent. They would marry several years later.

Who are we as a people? Amelia soon discovered that maybe the Emancipation Proclamation signed by Abraham Lincoln in 1863 didn't apply to most Blacks living in the Black Belt. This part of the country had been called the "Black Belt" because of the rich black soil that produced abundant cotton crops. In *Bridge Across Jordan,* Amelia pointed out that at the time, most Blacks in many parts of the country, and particularly in the southern states felt that the prevailing attitude was "White is Right," and this is what gave the white man right to lynch, to whip, to segregate, and to exploit.[12]

Several studies have shown that most blacks in this Great Depression era were persuaded to believe (even if subconsciously) only what the white man wanted them to believe. On the many large plantations found in Dallas County (a rural area) and other nearby counties, Blacks went to the fields early in the mornings and worked until dark and so had little or no time for them to attend school to learn writing, reading and basic arithmetic.

Most Black folks in southern states lived on property owned by plantation owners. Plantation owners would manage their own property or

---

[12] Ibid., 53.

let landlords oversee the property for sharecroppers where some tenants lived.

For some young school-age Blacks, part of their day was spent in school and the rest of the day they were out in the field picking cotton and managing farmland for the plantation owner. Some Blacks couldn't even attend school during the spring of the year because this was harvest time for cotton. And so there was no choice, but to return to school in the fall, as Amelia observed.

Robinson also noticed that blacks were either an asset or a liability to the owner when their land was sold to the next property owner. In Selma, she witnessed property owners who were proud of their sharecroppers as if they were a herd of cattle branded with great value.

In those days, landlords kept a tight grip on sharecroppers, by keeping them in debt through forcing them to take out loans for food, clothing and shelter. That way, Negroes never got caught up on their debts, continually owing the plantation owner, and thus making it easy for him to control them. In the 1930s, 1940s, and into the 1950s and even through the 1960s, plantation owners watched the growth of the Black boys and girls on their farms and encouraged mating with the hope that there would be more farmhands born who could work the fields and pick cotton. Plantation owners often went to far as to add an additional room onto the crowded sharecropper shacks in order to keep young couples on the land to work.

Who are "colored" folks as a people? That's the question Amelia continued to ask herself as she would soon hear the horror stories of cruel and inhumane treatment from sharecroppers and tenants who confided in her and husband Bill on a daily basis. She would often look up to the heavens and in her thoughts ask God, "Why?" What's the reason to let these human beings suffer like slaves at the beck and call of the 'Masas'" Her thinking was clear. These Black people down here in the heart of the South are truly living like slaves on a plantation. Amelia had no reason not to believe them because they were the same stories over and over again, with differences only in the details. She even learned that plantation owners would discourage Blacks from buying marriage licenses by persuading them that it was a waste of time and that he could perform the weddings just as a justice of the peace.

Later, Blacks would find out that the fabricated "marrying" by the plantation owner made it difficult to get certain benefits that required legal proof of marriage. Benefits like Social Security disability and retirement benefits were hard to get because Negroes could not prove that they were married nor were there any wages reported to the federal government to prove that they had been working.

In her diaries, Amelia described one incident involving a frail woman named Maria whom she had known since arriving in Selma. The story is both moving and heart-wrenching. Maria was a hard worker on a plantation owned by a doctor—a farm where she had lived her entire life. One day she came to Amelia frightened, fearing for her life. She had become a liability on the plantation because she wasn't able to produce the same amount of cotton that she had in the past.

In *Bridge Across Jordan,* Amelia noted that Maria had been one of the fastest cotton pickers on the plantation, picking as much as 400 pounds a day. Maria had explained to Amelia that everybody knew that a doctor had botched an operation on her and then refused to see her to fix it. Instead, he told this elderly lady to go home and lie down and die because it wouldn't be long before she passed away anyway.

As Amelia continued to watch Maria cry in fear, explaining how she returned to the doctor a few days later. Amelia tried to console Maria and tried to get her to stop crying and catch her breath because she felt that Maria was getting ready to pass out. A few minutes later, Maria took a deep breath and began to tell how the doctor just shoved her out of his office.

Tom Brown, who lived out on the other end of the plantation, came and told her that the doctor had offered him $10 if he would take Maria down by the Alabama River and drown her. With that inside information, Amelia wrote in *Bridge Across Jordan*: "We were able to help Maria. She had needed medical attention right away, and we asked churches and individuals to raise money for another operation. Maria was admitted into a hospital, where she received the proper care,"[13] After healing from surgery, Amelia along with others helped Maria move to another county.

---

[13] Ibid., 61.

CHAPTER 3
MID-TWENTIETH CENTURY, DALLAS COUNTY

It's important that young people know about the struggles we faced to get to the point we are today. Only then will they appreciate the hard-won freedom of blacks in this country.

—AMELIA BOYNTON ROBINSON

Selma, Lord, Selma, to say the least, was a new and quite interesting place. Amelia had to acclimate herself to a different environment and brand-new lifestyle that she knew nothing about. Up until her arrival, she had never heard of Selma, Alabama. The city would be a challenge for her. She arrived around the spring of 1930 in this small southern county known as "The Black Belt" because of its rich topsoil, which was ideal for growing cotton. Amelia's job was to teach the Black people of Dallas County, Alabama every phrase of home economics, which included cooking, cleaning, sewing, nutrition and other ways to maintain domestic household responsibilities.

Selma, Alabama was and is the county seat of Dallas County. Although

Abraham Lincoln had signed the Emancipation Proclamation in 1863, Amelia had faith that it was working and believed in it until coming to Dallas County, Alabama. Her eyes couldn't believe what she saw. It was as if the hands of time had gone backwards. Negroes were still enslaved by brainwashing from white supremacy shenanigans around the county and in the city of Selma.

She discovered that Blacks on most of the plantations were far from free. These poor people, she uttered, were afraid to speak up for themselves in fear of what the "white man" might do to them. Robinson observed that during this era of Jim Crow, Negroes particularly in Alabama, but also in many other parts of the country, were convinced and believed anything the white man told them. If "Massa" said it, then that's the way it is. At least subconsciously, this is what these "inferior" Black people were "hypnotized" to believe. Blacks also kept each other in bondage and oppression in small southern towns like Selma by not working together, trusting each other, or interacting by teaching each other how to read and write and count money.

For the most part, a lot of this slave mentality still exists today as a sort of undercurrent. An "Uncle Tom" mindset existed in Selma and throughout Alabama and other southern states up through the late 1960s. On large plantations and adjacent counties around the state there was no such thing as "normal working hours." The Negroes worked the fields and crops early in the morning until it was too dark to see. In her travels across the counties of Alabama, Amelia saw firsthand as a home economics teacher that there were still overseers who were as inhumane as slave-owners were during slavery. Consequently, to this day, a mark, or it could be called "a curse" remains on Black folks because at least psychologically some still haven't recovered from the injustices, including a sort of brainwashing, that had been inflicted upon their foreparents just three generations previously. In *Bridge Across Jordan,* Amelia noted her experiences of seeing plantation owners as proud of their sharecroppers as they were of a herd of cattle and the more that Blacks mated the more children there were to work the fields and pick cotton.

As was mentioned in the previous chapter, landlords also kept sharecroppers under their watch by offering signature loans on purchases of necessities like food, clothing, and shelter—all of which had to be purchased at the plantation. They would also promise Black families that working as sharecroppers would eventually lead to buying their way into owning the property lived on. Not so. This would never come to fruition because the plantation owner always found a loophole to keep them in debt. So, to Amelia, it really felt like the Emancipation Proclamation hadn't arrived in Selma. She observed that landlords even went the extra mile to keep young couples together on the property by adding a room to the already crowded shack their parents lived in. Furthermore, most of the time property owners decided when sharecroppers and their children could leave the property because they were treated as if they were indentured servants.

Bill and Amelia were told about a lot of cruel and inhumane treatment of sharecroppers in those days. Amelia had earned the trust of the Blacks in the surrounding rural communities of the county since she'd worked as a home demonstration agent for the federal government.

Although Blacks technically were free with civil rights, the Thirteenth Amendment, which ensured all rights for all people regardless of race, color and creed, had not yet arrived in Dallas County, Alabama. Blacks continued to be enslaved in the "Black Belt" counties from the 1930s, into the 1960s—almost as if no laws had been passed against the practice of slavery.

Obviously, formal southern confederacy states weren't ready to accept that Blacks were truly free and had all the civil rights and voting privileges enjoyed by Whites. And, in Selma and other rural counties, previously noted, records show that plantation owners discouraged Blacks from purchasing official marriage licenses and instead, they would act as justice of the peace. The could only give verbal consent, but would tell Black couples that they were married.

Second class citizenship was in full effect in Dallas County, including the city of Selma and all the rural community areas that Bill and Amelia represented at the time. History documents that plantation owners controlled when farm hands could go to the doctor, church, or even mate and marry. Because farmhands respected Amelia as a leader, these facts were often shared with her by sharecroppers because they felt she would and could help fight for their freedom.

During the Great Depression era Blacks in Dallas County suffered no differently than in previously years. Racism and discrimination were alive and well and blacks still unable to register and vote. Black and White churches were still separated and communication barriers still existed throughout the region. As Amelia Boynton recalls in *Bridge Across Jordan,* it would not be until 1968 that Protestant Christian groups would invite a Black or a group of Blacks to worship with them.

In 1936, Amelia resigned as home demonstration agent to marry

Samuel William "Bill" Boynton who was the county extension agent.

Having been taught by her parents that she was equal to Whites and not inferior to them, Amelia also had the advantage of growing up in Savannah, Georgia where she saw Blacks like her parents owning their own homes and farmland, having mortgage notes, and willpower planted in their minds to be and achieve whatever they desired to accomplish in life.

CHAPTER 4

STAY IN A "NIGGER'S" PLACE: A NEW ERA ON THE UP RISE

I had worse things than that done when I was fighting for people's right to vote. I have been called a rabble-rouser and an agitator. But because of my fighting, I was able to hand to the entire country the right for people to vote.

—AMELIA BOYNTON ROBINSON

Up until the latter part of the 1960s, Black folk in Selma were sharecroppers on White-owned plantations just to make ends meet. Whites across the South felt the pressure that Black people in Selma and surrounding counties and across the South were becoming restless in wanting to have all of their civil rights.

There were very few Blacks who lived in the city of Selma, whereas most had homes in Dallas County rural communities, working on plantations as sharecroppers and local farmhands. Blacks who were educated enough to stand up and fight against Jim Crow laws and make a difference in their city, did nothing of the kind. Instead, schools were segregated and Black educators who had graduated from Historical Black

Colleges and Universities (HBCUs) of the time were only allowed to teach their own people in separate schools where only Blacks attended with lesser curriculum to work with in educating young Blacks of school age.

Ministers, teachers, community grocery store owners and Black businesses knew their places in the town and made no effort to improve the situation for their neighbors who lived next door to them, or for those who continued to be sharecroppers on plantations. The reason for this is that they were afraid of being lynched, shot at, murdered, and bullied by the white man who labeled them as troublemakers. As documented throughout the history of America and as Robinson points out in *Bridge Across Jordan,* "Their thinking was 'White is right' and that gives the white man the privilege to lynch, to whip, to segregate and to exploit,"

Amelia Boynton Robinson shares an electrifying account from the early 1930s when she met a woman who had been shipped over from Sierra Leone in West African around the age of twelve in the 1860s. Sierra Leone had been a departure point for thousands of West African captives. She was known as Aunt Sally on the plantation where she lived as a sharecropper. Aunt Sally would tell Amelia stories of her native land and would sometimes speak in her mother tongue—which only her daughter and some grandchildren understood. When Amelia met her, Aunt Sally was still living in the same hut she settled in when brought to Dallas County, Alabama after arriving in America as an enslaved child. The hut was a tiny one-room, with a kitchen, but with no electricity or inside toilet. It was summertime and Amelia was making her rounds to the communities to have her monthly club meeting with the sharecroppers. This sunny day was different. The magnolia flowers were in full bloom and the green grass manicured with precision as if it could be sat on to enjoy the beams from the sun. But, as Robinson describes, she and Aunt Sally sat on a board that had been made from two old trees,. During their many conversations, Amelia tried to get in as many questions as she could because this would be the only person she would meet at this point who had come directly from Africa to be sold as a slave.

Aunt Sally began to act out her anguish to Amelia as if it came straight from a scenes in a motion picture. So, Robinson continues, "How did you get here in these parts of America?" Aunt Sally spoke with sadness, "I couldn't help myself. Africa was where I'm from and white man came to take it from us," she cried. She recalled her family and tribe members being shackled, whipped, chained and beaten down like animals. She began to recollect and sees her village on fire: all were weeping. She ran, but was caught and at first thought these people who had come to help.[14] "I fought but they beat me down, "explained Aunt Sally.

Then Aunt Sally began to go back in time again and spoke as if she were a child in her village playing around with the other kids having fun. She had grown up in her village around family members. It felt like time stood still as she talked of her father being one of the chiefs in the village. While thinking about the enslavement she'd had to endure in America, Aunt Sally reminisced that her village was clean, and there was laughter. Her people wove cloth from grass, took baths in the sun-lit river. There was no fighting, no beating, no killing.

She relived how they put everyone on a big ship with many tribe members. It seemed like weeks, months or maybe even a year had gone by. There was no walking around on the boat because they all had chains on

---

[14]Ibid., 67.

their feet.

With an expression of anxiety, Aunt Sally remembered a baby being born and the mother throwing him out to the fishes. She often dreamed of wanting to die with the hopes of waking up from the bad nightmare and finding that none of this was true.

As told by Aunt Sally, many died on the boat and flies covered their faces. The boat sometimes carried the stench of death as others began to die midway across the Atlantic because of the horrific living conditions the Africans endured throughout the crossing. Aunt Sally continued: White men would come down and make black men pick 'em up (the dead bodies) and throw 'em over in the water.[15] Upon arrival in Virginia Aunt Sally says the ship had to be cleaned up, and because there were no toilets, it was filthy, and the smell was enough to kill you. By now the scenes were vivid enough that anyone who didn't know what it was like traveling across the Atlantic Ocean to America on slave ships would have a picture of the horrors that transpired.

Many white men kept these Africans ("enslaved niggers") in check: with a whip and stick, and they were chain-bound to make sure no one escaped. More slaves were taken aboard in Virginia to replace the dead ones who had been thrown off the ship, Aunt Sally remembered. Aunt Sally told Amelia that there were many more deaths and the dead were tossed overboard right up until their arrival in Mobile, Alabama.

In Mobile Alabama, she was a twelve-year-old child and given to a man from South Africa—although she later found out she had a family. They

[15] Ibid., 68.

were sold on the block as man and wife, but they could not communicate because he was from South Africa and she was from West Africa. "We came to the Quarles plantation in this place called Bogue Chitto and here is where I've been ever since," Aunt Sally recounted.

The slave masters and overseers would continue to beat Aunt Sally and her husband for every little thing they didn't understand in English. Aunt Sally felt that the overseer was a bad man who wanted to beat on them all the time. She told Amelia that her husband was a good and wise man who took care of his family. After slavery, they became sharecroppers on the plantation.

Amelia's memoir summarizes Aunt Sally and her husband's contribution to America: It was the birth of one daughter, seven grandchildren, and a host of great-grandchildren. Amelia followed up with Sally's offspring in later years to discover that several became teachers, ministers, laborers, and housewives.

Robinson did find some comfort in looking back over her diary as she remembered that there was one other fact she wanted to mention about her visits with Aunt Sally. Maybe, she thought, one day she would be able to share with the world an astonishing story of a lady who endured the journey to America only to be enslaved and troubled for the rest of life because of the color of her skin.

Amelia continued to have strong ties with Tuskegee after graduating from there. Foreign students would come from all over the world to the United States, and black visitors were always sent to Tuskegee by the federal government for courses or training in various trades, particularly agriculture, since this was the Black Belt and the deep south was known for its rich soil for growing cotton, peanuts, corn, and various crops. Tuskegee would send the students to Dallas County to observe the systems used by the farmers and home demonstration agents.

By this time in 1936, Amelia had married Samuel William Boynton and had to relinquish her role as a home demonstration agent for Dallas County. In those days, getting married meant the end of extension work for women. Robinson says that it didn't matter how good a woman was at her job, the Extension Department could not see dividing an agent between her work and her husband.

Bill had already known the story of Aunt Sally and was aware she was born and reared in Sierra Leone, Africa up until the age of twelve. In 1936, Bill had a former classmate from Tuskegee visit him. His name was Daniel Kato from Sierra Leone, Africa. He was taken to meet Aunt Sally and they began to talk about Africa in general.

Abruptly, she screamed with happiness to find out the two of them were from the same tribe. Wow! What are the odds of that happening?

This would be the first time that Aunt Sally would meet someone from Africa who spoke and understood her language since leaving home more than 80 years earlier. They talked about their country, sometimes in their native tongue. Images of how clean the villages were kept came to mind, along with the nearby beauty of the rivers that flowed on the outskirts of the villages. Amelia saw and felt the joy in Aunt Sally's eyes and cried aloud with cheerfulness for her. This African woman never forgot her native land. Even though Aunt Sally never felt free, her emotions showed that she was emancipated.

During her years as the Dallas County extension agent, Amelia Boynton had made many black friends. One those friends would tell her exactly what went on in the white folks' house where she had been working for over 35 years. Flora explained being praised by one of the neighbors for extra work she had done for her. She told Flora's employer that her prayer was that God would take Flora to heaven when she dies.

Her employer butt in with, "Do you think God has niggers in His heaven? If I thought that God had black niggers up there, I wouldn't want to go." The neighbor lady replied with, "Why do you think God has children that he does not love? Blacks are as much human beings and the handiwork of God as we are. He has no prejudice as you and I have, my friend. Certainly, Blacks will go to heaven when they die.[16]

Flora's employer had been a prominent person at the church she belonged to, and a Bible class had been named in honor of her deceased husband. Amelia voiced in *Bridge Across Jordan* that her friend Flora's employer replied, "Well if this is true, I'm through with God and his niggers and his heaven."

---

[16] Ibid., 74.

Chapter 5
EMANCIPATE, "HUMAN RIGHTS"

I was taught to love people, to excuse their hate, and realize that if they get the hate out of them, that they will be able to love. Only when all human beings begin to recognize themselves as human beings will prejudice be gone forever. People ask me what race I am, but there is no such thing as race. I just answered, I'm a member of the human race.

—Amelia Boynton Robinson

Well settled in now, Amelia called Selma home. Her family at this time consisted of five: husband Bill and herself, two sons—Bill Jr., Bruce, and a young lady named Leathia who had lived with Robinson before she was married. Bill and Amelia would attempt to help her go to college, but with only one income in the household now, it was impossible to keep Leathia in college. The Boyntons paid for one semester and asked the president of Tuskegee to put her on an extended plan so she could work her way through school. However, the school's five-year program was filled and Leathia could not be accepted on any plan.

Robinson writes in her autobiography *Bridge Across Jordan* that Dr. F.

D. Patterson, Tuskegee President, had been asked to send a girl to work at the governor's mansion in Montgomery. Leathia was recommended and accepted right away. The plan was for her to work a year to get enough money to return to school. She was only supposed to work at the governor's mansion as supervisor in the housework, but instead multiple duties were given to assist in all kinds of work.

The governor's wife gave the instructions and the black servants obeyed. As time passed, Leathia became comfortable with her duties and decided to take the initiative to make the necessary preparations for the dignitaries' arrival for dinner. The governor's wife had no tolerance for her black servants taking any initiative or responsibility to do anything.

Robinson remembers the story as it was told to her by Leathia: The governor's wife had stopped what she was doing, Leathia explained. "You thought? Who are you? You are not supposed to think," the governor's wife said. "You are a nigger, and hereafter I am to do the thinking here."[17] She ordered that the things be put back into place. But less than an hour later, she returned and directed Leathia to arrange things exactly as she had done earlier. Leathia continued to work there despite the governor's wife's treatment of her and the other black servants.

After coming home one weekend, Leathia was sick at heart and filled with disgust over all she'd seen while working at the governor's mansion. She had an awful time fighting off many of the white men who sought out sex from her. One of the older female black servants explained to her that this was a common custom. With this and all the other ill-mannered

---

[17] Ibid., 71.

discussion at the table after dinner. Leathia left with no notice that she was leaving for good.

Many more incidents occurred during the Great Depression era when blacks and whites in the South would attempt to connect in the hope of resolving the discrimination and segregation that harmed both races.

With no compromise in sight the "good" white citizens continued to justify to themselves that Blacks were inferior to them in the Black Belt, put a stop to the mingling of the races, and continued to suppress the black vote. Whites were ostracized if they fellowshipped with black Christians who belonged to the same organizations in some sections of Selma. No Protestant Christian group would invite Blacks to worship with them or take part in their discussions. It would not be until 1968 when change would occur in any of these areas where an affiliation between the white and black ministerial groups would begin to associate and communicate.

There were missionary groups and the Selma City Federation of Clubs in the 1930s and 1940s that were part of a national organization whose purpose was deal with different subjects of national interest. "Amelia Boynton" church organizations continued to invite Whites because the black Christians realized that along the colored lines someone needed to break down segregation or at least make the best effort.

CHAPTER 6
PROGRAMING OF BLACK PEOPLE

The Blacks would gather downtown from the outlying farms every Saturday in Selma like it was a big picnic. You weren't allowed to drink from the 'white' water fountain, and police officers would pace the streets, pushing the colored people with cattle prods.

They were so frightened and conditioned to be subservient; they'd just move out of their way.

—AMELIA BOYNTON ROBINSON

Bill and Amelia Boynton realized that a lot of work would need to be done to convince Blacks in Dallas County and surrounding rural communities and the city of Selma that they had just as much civil and equal rights to be in this country as any other person regardless of their race or the color of their skin. It was 1936 and Amelia resigned as home demonstration agent to marry Bill. She and Bill would spend the next three decades fighting for voting and property ownership rights for black residents. Yes, Blacks were emancipated, but in the southern states it had not caught on just yet. Jim Crow existed to keep Blacks from voting, and forcing segregation in restaurants, theaters, schools, and bathrooms.

The Boyntons now had a son and Amelia began to work for an insurance company. It became difficult for Amelia to find someone to keep their son because Blacks did not like working for other Blacks and did less work as compared to working for Whites, Amelia points out in *Bridge Across Jordan.* She learned from her housekeepers that they were getting paid less working for white people than they would be working for them.

This would go on for a while as Amelia would employ black women to work in their house only to have them leave after an offer was made from a white family to work for them. She soon learned that these black women were getting paid lesser than what she was offering, even though they would have more work and responsibilities working for Whites. Most Blacks in the Dallas County area had been born on plantations as had their parents and foreparents before them, representing generations being brainwashed.

In what way were they brainwashed? They were made to feel inferior to white people, not wanting to learn to read or write, with no desire or felt-need for school because it had been drilled into their minds by their parents that the master was going to take care of them. Therefore, most black folk grow up illiterate. Even the black ministers feared what "Mr. Charlie" would do to him if he found out that Blacks on the plantation were being exposed to knowledge they were not to know.

Amelia witnessed that plantation owners had many of these backwoods country preachers under control. All sermons and political views were passed through the masters first for approval and if there was any notion of arousing the sharecroppers, it would be removed from the messages. Years later, in 1967, Amelia would visit one of these churches that had existed in the 30s, 40s, and 50s in the rural area outside of Selma only to find that black churches were still being governed by plantation owners to control what ministers were teaching the congregation on their land.

In the 30s and 40s, Amelia Boynton had a chance to fight against segregation: the hatred, hostility and fear. Just listening to her remember and talk about some of the injustices gave a glimpse into what it was like to witness the wickedness and evil of segregation against the black race. She would experience the same racism through slander and prejudiced remarks when shopping at the local furniture, grocery, and appliance stores in Selma. During the Great Depression and on throughout World War II, Amelia Boynton would stand her ground, remembering the principles she was taught as a child and that she had rights as a law-abiding citizen. As segregated as Dallas County, Alabama was during this era, Amelia Boynton commanded respect from the local merchants and demanded that whomever she did business with show respect by referring to her as a customer or by the title she would prefer.

The Boyntons played a key role in desegregating one of the most racist areas in the United States, namely Dallas County, Alabama. Amelia Boynton would play a pivotal role in making this happen. At times as a role play, she would act out the character of an uneducated black woman with the objective of showing how white people think and maneuver to continually make blacks feel inferior to them in the city of Selma and in more rural areas of the county.

Amelia felt that there simply was no justification for black people having separate bathrooms from Whites, or separate schools, separate waiting rooms at doctor's offices and hospitals, simply because of skin color. Most Blacks were afraid to stand up and speak to white people in the Deep South, and especially in Dallas County. It all goes back to enslaved Africans coming to America being brainwashed into believing that slavery still existed under the Jim Crow laws. Former Confederacy southern states created those laws to keep Blacks under their control after the Emancipation Proclamation. Although southern states were part of the Union, unlike the northern states, whites still wanted to hold on to their slaves through Jim Crow. Blacks would now become enslaved as sharecroppers living on plantations that were owned by former slave owners. These plantations would be managed and set up in a way that made Blacks "servants" who lived on the "master's" land in shabby, old, run-down wooden shacks while still working their way toward a freedom that some still felt didn't happen until civil and voting rights laws were passed in the 1960s. Under Jim Crow, black children living on plantations would get schooling three to four months out of the year, while unfortunately, the rest of the year was spent working in the fields picking cotton. This would leave them uneducated, and with the handicap of being unable to read or write in adulthood.

CHAPTER 7
CIVIL RIGHTS ACTIVISTS, THE BOYNTONS

I was born to lead.

—AMELIA BOYNTON ROBINSON

I will fight for Negroes until I die, for Negroes really don't know they should be free. They don't know their strength, but once they know it, this will be a different section in which to live. They will be happier because I have put myself out on a limb for them.

—SAMUEL BOYNTON

Amelia was led into leadership roles at a young age. As a child, she saw leadership in her parents. While growing up in a two-story wooden house in Savannah, Georgia, her father owned a wholesale wood lot. She notes in *Bridge Across Jordan* that she had an instinct for leadership in her DNA from birth. The community expected also expected this of the Boyntons' household. Amelia was introduced to politics at the age of ten while traveling by horse and buggy with her mother who was committed to the women's suffrage movement. Amelia enjoyed knocking on doors and ringing doorbells in so she could give women the information they needed to go to the registration board or polls to cast their votes.

Samuel William (Bill) Boynton should be included as an important figure in American history books because of his efforts in fighting for full citizenship for African Americans, as well as his life-long devotion to improve the economic and political situation for black people. Bill was born in Griffin, Georgia in 1904, and graduated from Tuskegee Institute in Agricultural Science. He arrived in Dallas County, Alabama in 1928 as a county agent for the Alabama Extension Service.

It was in 1930 when Bill would meet his future wife Amelia Platts. Bill would hold voter registration drives for Blacks in Selma from the 1930s to the early 1960s until his death. The Boyntons realized early on that Blacks in Selma and the Dallas County rural areas felt like they weren't citizens since less than one percent of them were registered voters. The population of Blacks in this area around the time of the Great Depression was approximately 15,000, while it is estimated that the number of registered black voters around 300.

As president of registration and voting of his congressional district, Bill and Amelia are credited for laying the groundwork for the Voting Rights Act. One of Boyntons' key roles would be to convince local Blacks that they were not servants, but instead were indeed citizens with voting rights in America. He would continually teach Blacks how to farm and buy land so they could work for themselves in order to avoid unfair working conditions, and become economically self-sufficient.[18] Bill would travel

[18] SNCCDigitalGateway.

down dusty dirt roads deep in the rural and backwoods of the county teaching Black people better methods of farming, as well as how to gain political, financial and educational strength[19]

He was repeatedly made aware of the political pressure fighting against him in his struggle for the rights of the African American community and this would eventually take a toll on his health. Bill resigned as the county agent in 1953 before being fired for standing up for voting and civil rights for Blacks. Bill was president of the Fourth Congressional District for Registration and Voting from 1945 until his death in 1963.

He realized that his district, which included Dallas, Autauga, Coosa, Calhoun, Talladega, St. Clair, Etowah, and Clay counties, had only 1,005 Blacks registered to vote as compared to 175,000 Whites who were registered voters. This disparity remained until the Civil Rights Voting Act was passed in 1965.[20]

In the 1940s, Bill and Amelia would take their fight for voting rights to Washington D.C. to ask their congressman to vote so that the voting rights bill would be taken out of its holding pattern so it could be voted on. However, their congressman refused to assist them in getting the bill to the floor for a vote

[Note: In 1955, S.W. Boynton testified before a U.S Senate subcommittee concerning the denial of the franchise to Blacks in Alabama. This testimonial would become instrumental in the passage of the 1957

---

[19]Famous People Biographies. "Sam Boynton Biography."
https://famousbiographies.org/sam-boynton-biograph

[20] Ibid., 111.

Civil Rights Act].

Bill would receive the Merit Award from Tuskegee in 1940. At this time, it would be the highest honor given to a graduate of the university.

Bill's contribution to the Dallas County community included helping to assist in the purchase of 120 acres of land, building 4-H centers for African Americans and securing monies for the building of the Colored Community Center in the 1940s. A bust of Mr. Boynton stands in the Alabama 4-H Center in Columbiana, Alabama honoring his commitment to helping the underprivileged and disenfranchised. Another of Bill's accomplishments in the 1940s involved establishing a recreational center named "Joyland," which was located on the outskirts of Selma.

Bill would not live to see the equality for Blacks that he had worked toward so faithfully. The stress from fighting to educate sharecroppers about their rights so they could achieve economic self-sufficiency seriously taxed the Boyntons' marriage. This was compounded by threats from white supremacy groups like the Ku Klux.

Years after Bill's death, the S.W. Boynton Lay Justice Award would be established by The Alabama Lawyers Association to represent Mr. Samuel W. Boynton for his service as a lay advocate in the black community during a time of harsh discrimination. Historical records also show that Mr. Boynton was recognized as a Selma resident who not only laid the historical foundation for the Voting Rights Act, but who also invited the first black lawyers into the Black Belt in order to pursue civil rights cases.

The Boyntons would empower blacks in the urban and rural communities to work for themselves in order to avoid the unfair working conditions forced upon them by white plantation owners. Bill would pass away from a heart attack in Selma May 1963, yet, Amelia vowed to carry on the fight for equal voting and civil rights for black people.

The couple defied the southern system of racism from the 1930s until the Student Nonviolent Coordinating Committee (SNCC) came to Selma in 1964. Civil Rights activist Bill Boynton and his wife Amelia led black voter registration drives and hosted the Student Nonviolent Coordinating Committee in Selma, Alabama. SNCC would teach Blacks to how own land and how to register to vote.

CHAPTER 8
HATRED - "BLACK LIVES MATTER"

I was taught to love people, to excuse their hate and realize that if they get the hate out of them, that they will be able to love.

—AMELIA BOYNTON ROBINSON

Okay! Let's consider it as heard and seen through the eyes of Amelia Boynton Robinson. She understood Selma was notorious for beating and brainwashing black folks into believing that "White is Right" and "Black is Wrong." There is no doubt that after Amelia had lived in the city for a few years, she realized that Dallas County had an unusual protocol and an "antique" sense of itself. This would be during the Great Depression era when Blacks would be jailed for looking at a white person in a way that scared them into believing that a nigger was getting ready to attack them. All a white person had was say that a Black was looking at them the wrong way, or that a group of them were huddling up together to plan something, or maybe a black person didn't address them properly. This could be cause for some sort of disciplinary action such as jail time or maybe just a good beating. As told by Amelia in *Bridge Across Jordan,* some Blacks, having committed no crime, would be kept in jail with no charges for several weeks, only to be released once the room and board for the stay in jail had been paid by the incarcerated person. In the 1930s, through the 1950s, it would be nothing to find a black person in Selma getting an ass-whoopin', a lynching or be killed by a white person. There would be other stories of Blacks being beaten, dragged, hugged, buried alive or shot to death by Whites in Selma.

By now, the Boyntons had made friends with residents and sharecroppers from time spent in their county extension work. And word had soon gotten around that Amelia and Bill were educated, could be trusted, and were people who had their best interests in mind. Dallas County and local Selma city residents would come to the Boyntons, sharing their horror stories of ill treatment as African Americans at the hands of sharecroppers and landlords over the plantations. Bill and Amelia would help church ministers, African Americans and anyone else who sought their help to escape the hands of death, bondage, and beating from white people in Dallas County.

In *Bridge Across Jordan,* Amelia shares that when an officer of the law said he had killed a Black, he would be justified because the law was on his side and it was always open season in Selma for African Americans to be killed by officers enforcement.[21] These vicious crimes would be carried out in Dallas County and in the city of Selma for the next three decades. No doubt African Americans were afraid for their lives and for their children's.

---

[21] Ibid., 123.

How else could it be explained that Blacks would watch family members lynched, beaten and even killed without reporting it to the authorities? It's obvious that Jim Crow laws were effect in the South and at this point in time, there was no way that Whites would be willing to give up their slavery mentality to do what was right under laws of the United States of America. It was a known fact that blacks in these deep-rooted southern racist formal confederacy states like Alabama, Mississippi, and Georgia failed to follow the Emancipation Proclamation by making Jim Crow the new law of the land for the enslavement of black folks by way of sharecropping.

Where is justice? When would this senseless violence and racism that took place just because a person's skin was "colored" rather than White ever end? Amelia and Bill could not believe what they had experienced in Selma. There were man-made rules set up in the city that black people instinctively knew they had to follow. They knew that if they spoke out of character about the way city or the county ran things, the consequences could include being beaten, lynched or killed just because they were not staying in a "niggard's" place.

Amelia and Bill were aware of almost every major court case in the city that centered on blacks. The couple would defy the odds and get involved in cases where they felt that the person on trial was not guilty and they thought the case might be winnable. They would also give legal guidance to those that needed it. Two court cases Amelia that wrote about in *Bridge Across Jordan* involved African Americans, and a white jury and judge.

One of the verdicts was against two black teenage boys who were sentenced to 30 years in prison for peppering two white men who had beaten their mother because she wouldn't tell them her son's whereabouts. This involved two brothers who didn't chop cotton on a Saturday because after working hard in the cotton field all week long, they felt they deserved a day off. The sharecropper became angry because the two boys talked back to him and refused to work.

The second court case evolved around an elderly woman around the age of 70-year-old woman getting beaten to death in her own house by an officer of the law because she had forbidden her granddaughter from seeing the white officer. The granddaughter had been sent away by her grandmother so that her night-time "integration" with the white officer would stop. After the beating the old woman, she tried to run out the front door, but the office knocked her out with the butt of his pistol, threw her off the porch, and shot her in the lower abdomen. She died instantly.

Amelia vividly remembered in *Bridge Across Jordan* that the officer who had killed the elderly woman was calm, cool, and at ease as he sat in the courtroom awaiting his verdict. Some witnesses were called to the stand, but not the defendant. In their summary to the jury, the lawyers for the defense said, "Gentleman, this was a poor, old, ignorant nigger. Her days were just about done. She had nothing to offer the world." Amelia understood him to be saying that old black people are rejects and worn out laborers. And, if that weren't enough, the lawyer continued by saying, "Gentlemen, if you find this officer of the law—this fine, promising gentleman, this white man, guilty, then no white man will have the freedom to go to any nigger's house."[22]

---

[22] Ibid., 126.

The jury verdict came back in the defendant's favor: not guilty. Roaring with anger, Amelia asked herself how for God's sake the man could not be guilty when his uniform, gun and shoes were spattered and soaked with the blood of the dead woman. Damn! Damn! Damn!

Amelia reacted to the decision with anguish and disbelief, but didn't expose her reaction or thoughts of being "pissie" mad to the judge, jurors or lawyers. She had lost all faith in the justice system and the white man for now. She felt that all white people were no good racists and wished that there were somewhere to go where no white people existed.

Amelia Boynton would show her anger against whites and the court system in Selma by crying and venting at home, as she laid across her bed asking God aloud where justice was and why He allowed this to happen. As Amelia continued to sob on her bead, the doorbell rang and her not to her liking—it was a priest from the Fathers of St. Edmund's (a black parish). He was white and this didn't please Amelia Boynton at all, but because of her upbringing, she was hospitable.

Obviously, she felt, the priest could tell her eyes were watery from crying. Amelia explained that she had just returned from the courthouse and was upset because justice had not been done to the officer who shot and murdered the seventy-year-old lady. Speaking in a soft soothing voice, he assured Mrs. Boynton that not all white people were not like that. Amelia lashed out and said there are no good white people when it comes to black people.

She asked him to clarify how it could be that white folks in this city could watch other whites murder black just because their skin color. Where was the justice in that? In his comforting voice, the priest told Amelia to just give it time and allow God to prevail.

"Time, hell!" Amelia shouted out. How much time would be needed before justice prevailed? It had been several hundred years and still there was no justice. If a white man or woman were beating a colored woman on Broad Street and this violent act went to court, the side of that white man or woman would be prevail, even if it were obvious that the black woman were innocent. She was convinced that the priests in the town were just as bad as anyone else because they just sat back and said nothing if it looked what they said might be in a black person's favor. "The only good white man is a dead one,"[23] Amelia says. He looked at her in despair and muttered that Mrs. Boynton could cry to get out the pain, but cautioned her that being angry would not help the situation at all. He left after giving his lecture without uttering another word.

Soon Bill came home. He had already heard about the all-white jury and judge verdict and the sentences (that the white police officer was acquitted of all charges). Bill realized Amelia had been crying and how much these new injustices had affected her. Bill began consoling her while at the same time cautioning her about how wrong it was to hate white people. He explained to Amelia that her heart had hardened and appeared to be just as bad or worse than those that hand out injustices to black people. As Amelia digested what Bill had said, she realized that she was destroying herself and becoming worse than those who had been killing black folks in Selma just because they hated niggers.

This would be a new beginning in Amelia's life in that seeking to understand why white people hated blacks so much would become her new mission. She was determined to learn how to communicate more

[23] Ibid., 128.

effectively with White, and would even study them in order to be knowledgeable and so she could look at them as her sisters and brothers. In later years, Amelia would learn to pity white bigots because she felt it was an emotional sickness that must be treated with compassion and empathy.

CHAPTER 9
THE BOYNTONS' OFFICE

You can never know where you are going unless you know where you have been.

—AMELIA BOYNTON ROBINSON

It was the 1950s and two decades had passed since Selma was home for the Boyntons. While no longer teaching and traveling around the rural areas of Dallas County as a home demonstrator, the friendships made over the years endured for Amelia. It was clear how much they respected and trusted the Boyntons in both the city and in the rural areas of the county. Bill and Amelia had become business savvy as self-employed entrepreneurs and their office in Selma had become a place where Blacks could vent about the problems and injustices happening within the black community. Other than the black educators, schoolteachers, and ministers, the Boyntons were more advanced in education and technical skills than most black folks in those days when Jim Crow was the law of the land in the Selma area.

From the 1940s through the mid-60s, the Boyntons' office housed a real estate company, an employment service, and a notary, as well as community and insurance services. All were designed to serve blacks in the community and it didn't matter whether you were well-to-do, rich, poor, intelligent or illiterate as all who needed help came to the office.

Their offices were used as a headquarters from 1963 to 1965 by civil rights workers, celebrities and citizens who sacrificed their everyday normal lives to contribute towards the soon-to-be movement for voting rights. And, the Boyntons' home, which was located at 1315 Lapsley Street, would become headquarters for Reverend Dr. Martin Luther King Jr. and the Southern Christian Leadership Conference (SCLC). The Student Nonviolent Coordination Committee was also a major American civil rights organization that helped the African American communities in Selma and the Dallas County in soliciting for the right to register and vote.

SNCC became one of the first organizations to set up shop in Selma in order to determine what the next movement should be in helping Blacks fight for the right to vote. At first they were reluctant in bringing the movement to Selma because blacks there feared for their lives because of White racism. Their biggest fears included being beat up, lynched, or blackballed in the city for raising up and balking against the Jim Crow system that had controlled African Americans in the state of Alabama for over a century. SNCC participated and helped in coordinating a lot of the marches from Brown Chapel Church to downtown Selma's Dallas County Courthouse in the push for the right to vote.

Yes! Jim Crow ruled, but somehow blacks in Selma maintained businesses in an area of downtown where few Whites were ever seen. Whether it be hot or cold weather on Saturdays, Blacks from both the city and rural areas would crowd the Boyntons' offices for help with real estate and insurance.

Many elderly Blacks also came to get help with their birth certificate records and assistance with filing income taxes. These senior citizens had hopes of someday applying for Social Security benefits. Unfortunately, it wouldn't help many of them because their work had never been recorded and their employers had never provided for old age pension in any way that could be proven by anyone. For example, many employer owned plantations where many blacks would live and work as sharecroppers working the crops and picking cotton for wages. And some would be domestic employees where cooking, ironing, cleaning for white people would be paid in cash.

On Saturday's, when blacks would gather in downtown Selma, white policemen would patrol the area heavily with loaded pistols and night sticks, knocking blacks out of the way when they didn't move fast enough. Black dared to talk back in protest, knowing that they would be slammed in jail on disorderly conduct charges as observed by Bill and Amelia.

Amelia would image a time when the poor white man, the black man, the red man, and others who had been denied freedom would combine strengths to change the course of American history. She would work to rectify the wrongs in the way society had treated Negroes through discrimination, segregation, and exploitation, and replace them with civil rights.

Since Selma would become, as some say, the cradle of the voting rights movement, black leaders in the 1920s would encourage African Americans to see that they were taxpayers and citizens who have the right to vote. But for the most part, they didn't believe this to be true in Selma and Dallas

County's rural areas. Jim Crow was in full effect and was deeply embedded southern region of racism and segregation. Southern Blacks in Selma and all over Alabama were afraid to stand up and speak out for fear of being whipped, lynched or experiencing other repercussions at the hands of white people.

For many years, Bill and Amelia urged black citizens to speak up and demand that the local government give them both respect and equal civil rights treatment. No results would come until 1965 since most Blacks in Selma had been brainwashed to believe that they were inferior to Whites in the community. And until this day, some still believe this falsehood to be true. In the latter part of 1920s, a group of Selma and Dallas County Blacks aimed to form the first city-county organization with one mission—becoming registered voters. But the Dallas County Voters' League (DCVL) diminished for lack of interest.[24]

In 1936, DCVL would be revived again when Bill would call members Mr. Charles J. Adams, Henry Boyd, and P.L. Lindsey. Again, DCVL would remain dormant because black folks were all about pleasing white folks because if they didn't, then their lives would be in danger. Adams, the elected president and founder in the 1920s, would be forced to leave Selma as he was in jeopardy of losing his railroad clerk job. Whites would pressure Adams to dismantle the DCVL, but Bill became head of the League until his death in 1963.

---

[24] Ibid., 136-137.

CHAPTER 10
VOTER SUPPRESSION

"A vote-less people is a hopeless people." There was a sign with these exact words posted in the window of our office. My husband Bill created this motto. He would cement them into the minds and hearts of everyone upon conversation with them.

—AMELIA BOYNTON ROBINSON

Bill would work hard as the DCVL president to get blacks registered to vote. But the county, city, and state worked harder to throw up even higher barriers to the black vote by making registration virtually impossible. In 1963, statistics showed there were only 180 registered black voters in Dallas County, even though approximately 15,000 blacks lived in the city and county areas at this time. Voting sites had been set up in these areas in order to assist Blacks in registering for several years prior. The Reverend Dr. Frederick D. Reese speaks about this in his book *Selma's Self-Sacrifice* and noted that Amelia and Sam Boynton were registered voters as far back as the late 1930s. "Amelia Boynton and her husband Sam dedicated themselves to encouraging blacks in Selma to reach for the stars and refrain from allowing oppressors to block their achievements."[25]

For many years prior to the arrival of the Boyntons to Selma, African Americans had been made aware that as taxpayers and citizens they had a right to vote. But whether it be the poor, middle or even upper class—Blacks didn't question the local government about voting rights in fear for their lives if they dared to rebel against the white supremacy system. No significant results would be seen until 1965.

Amelia gave a respectable interpretation of the right-to-vote battles leading up to the 1960s victory. She articulated that in 1867-68, men were the only ones allowed to vote. It would not be until the early 1920s women were given the right to vote. But during this time, there were many Negroes who realized the urgency of fighting for justice and their constitutional rights in the United States. In the late nineteenth century, Blacks began to register in large numbers, gaining a stronghold in political positions across the country. As Amelia pointed out, they would become mayors, congressmen and senators,.[26]

In 1910, Jim Crow would be in full force in southern states where hurdles to keep colored people from becoming voters prevailed, causing few Black to register. However, the Boyntons didn't let this stop them from teaching Blacks in the rural area of Dallas County, as well as the city of Selma how to fill out the one and one-half page application. This would need to be done at night, in the churches where lamp-lights were used and

[25] Frederick D. Reese and Kathy M. Walters, Selma's Self-Sacrifice (Printed in the United States of America, 2018), 205.
[26] Katherine Notley, "A Vote-Less People Is a Hopeless People." Executive Intelligence Review. March 18, 2005. https://larouchepub.com/other/interviews/2005 /3211amelia.html.

in the Boyntons' office on Saturdays. There were signs in the Boyntons' office which read, "If you have not made an attempt to register and vote, don't talk politics in here," and another sign they had was, "A vote-less people is a hopeless people," she said.

On the other hand, Amelia and Bill had no problems voting. Because Amelia worked for the federal government, she encountered no problems in registering to vote even at 21 years old. Bill was the county agent and a registered voter from when he was working in Georgia.

On the other hand, in the city of Selma up, Blacks had been conditioned with fear and fear is what kept them from speaking up or doing anything out of line that might displease white folks. "We were able to get the people who were in the rural district," explained Amelia.[27]

Colored folks in the South who lived and worked on farms as sharecroppers soon realized that their situations were hopeless without a voice to vote. So, Negroes living in the rural districts begin to speak out and encouraged others to register to vote.

Unfortunately, a pattern of voter suppression tactics would be visible throughout the 30s into the mid-60s. The Boyntons tried to help Blacks navigate through plight by convincing those throughout the city and county that standing up to vote was a right of first-class citizenship and a path out of Jim Crow Syndrome.

Disenfranchisement concerning voting rights after World War II could be seen as black soldiers returned home to Alabama and tried to register to

---

[27] Ibid.

vote. They would be deliberately ignored at the courthouse while whites who came into the office would be greeted by the registrar. A white person would be provided with the paperwork and promptly registered to vote. On the other hand, blacks would be ignored and overlooked while standing in line. Sometimes they would be called out by something other than their names in order to discourage them from voting with questions like "What you want boy?" and "What can I help you with nigger?" Then he would say, "You're disqualified. You didn't answer the question."

Of course, many wouldn't get past these racist tactics, and so they had to leave before going through the literacy and writing test. Those who did make it through the testing often had their registrations wadded up and thrown in the wastebasket.[28] This would play out over and over in registrars' offices across the South.

Data have shown that by 1953, in the Deep South, eleven counties where the black population equaled or exceeded that of whites, only 1.3% of all eligible Blacks registered to vote. Statistics show that two of these counties had no African American voters at all.[29] Other challenges the Boyntons faced in their persistence to make sure black folks had voting rights was their encounter with the poll tax—which all eleven states of the former Confederacy had adopted. The poll tax was cumulative and had a feature that made it effectively impossible to pay. For every year a person was eligible to vote, a payment was due. So, for example, if after twenty-five years of not voting or not being able to vote, an African American in

[28] Carol Anderson. One Person, No Vote: How Voter Suppression Is Destroying Our Democracy
[29] Ibid.

Alabama in the mid-1940s was finally able to pay the tax, he or she have a tax of not just $1.50, but rather it would be $37.50. By design, those back taxes effectively suppressed the black turnout.[30] On January 23, 1964, the United States ratified the 24th Amendment to the Constitution, prohibiting any poll tax in elections for federal officials.

---

[30] Ibid.

CHAPTER 11
INFERIORITY COMPLEX, CHATTEL SLAVERY

The white man, as a rule, has always tried to keep the African American in his place, like a robot who would come at his call. Those who would keep him ignorant are also the first to say the African American is incompetent, incapable, shiftless, and lazy.

—AMELIA BOYNTON ROBINSON

It was the mid twentieth century and Jim Crow was the law of the land in "the dirty south." Civil and voting rights were at forefront.

Education, or the lack thereof, continued to handicap Blacks. And Amelia would see that black schools in Dallas County and throughout the state of Alabama were inferior as they remained segregated, and understaffed with rundown, crumbling buildings. The school year was only three months long, as boys nine years of age and older were needed to work the fields and pick cotton during peak seasons. Most wouldn't receive anything approaching a good education for this reason. Eventually, many boys and girls, whose parents lived in rundown shacks, would drop out of school completely by tenth grade.

Then there would be the inferiority complex reinforced by then Governor George Wallace. Wallace would put up every hurdle he could possibly think of because he saw that blacks were fighting for civil rights and the right to vote. Amelia noted that Wallace had one time even said, "Segregation today, segregation tomorrow, segregation forever."[31] In 1963, he defied the federal government by standing in the door at the Foster Auditorium, keeping two African American students, Vivian Malone and James Hood, from entering.

The disenfranchisement in education for blacks in Dallas County and across the state of Alabama can be seen in black teachers who held a bachelor or master degrees, and even those working toward doctorates. It also could be seem with new college graduates who were teaching for the first time being taken out of their fields of study, and even those who had been teaching for many years were sometimes forced to teach other subjects. Amelia added that this meant these teachers had to work overtime to prepare and the school did not have the benefit of that teacher's previous experience. [32]

African American renters or landowners would try to keep their boys in school until they closed. But for the most part, they made sacrifices in order to send their children into the city so they could get nine months of schooling, Amelia recalled.[33]

---

[31] Notley.

[32] Boynton Robinson, 151.

[33] Ibid., 152.

Schools in the city and rural counties endured tremendous duress during the 1950s due to a lack of school equipment and teaching supplies needed for black students who were achievers with a high aptitude. These students sat on hard benches chiseled out of lumber, in classrooms that were often built out of weatherboarding, fueled by wood for light. Mrs. Lorene Stewart, who had a master's degree and taught in schools like this until the 1960s, recounted to Amelia how she used pasteboard boxes to keep the schoolroom warm.[34]

Classrooms would be overcrowded, with some county schools having nearly 600 students, with arrangements for five classrooms having five teachers dividing the students amongst themselves. At a club meeting for teachers that Amelia attended, she voiced her opinion about the deterioration of the black schools versus the nice pleasant atmosphere of a white school she had visited. Her discussion with the teachers resulted in a heated debate, with half of the members favoring Amelia's lecture on the black poor school system, and the other half not approving.

In 1954, the Supreme Court ruled to desegregate schools. However, both state and local officials deceived Blacks in Dallas County, resulting in schools remaining segregated.

The white man's treatment of Blacks under Jim Crow and white supremacy mentality can be seen further when considering how the Boyntons were treated as entrepreneurs in owning their own life and fire insurance company. An elderly man named George Tate, who owned and operated one of the largest real estate agencies in Selma, despised the idea

---

[34] Ibid., 153.

of the African Americans like the Boyntons having businesses like a white man.

Most white folk wouldn't show their true colors, but instead they would keep it to themselves a tolerate Niggers on the "down low." George Tate couldn't bear this burden any longer, so he picked a suitable time to unleash his fury on Bill on the day he had gotten out of the hospital and returned to the office.

Amelia expounds that Tate walked into the office and bust out, "You dirty, lowdown, black nigger. I hate you. I am going to take this stick and kill you." Bill was surprised and didn't understand what was going on as he had never met Tate before. Tate was as drunk as a skunk, and he started to strike Bill with his cane. Amelia jumped up and grabbed it from him. Amelia felt that if Bill had not been there, she would have given Tate a good beating. She was ready to hit him, but Bill talked her out of it.[35] Bill said the man was sick with hate and prejudice. His mind and soul were germinated.

When Tate to the street, both blacks and whites were laughing at him. He retaliated by beating the front glass door down from top to bottom. By the time the police arrived, he had finished the job. Amelia notes that if he had come back into the office that this would have been one day that she had not practiced nonviolence.

No black lawyers would take their case for fear of retribution from white folks that would impact their livelihood. There was the pervasive "White is Right" and "Black is (always) wrong" mentality. This

---

[35] Ibid., 166.

indoctrination had been perpetrated by the so-called "good white-folks" for more than 300 years, Amelia noted.

Not only did the Boyntons endure hate from white folk, but they experienced fear and alienation even from those of their own color. Many Blacks had insurance policies with the Boyntons, but some feared to talk with them outside of their office. They did not think that the Boyntons were talking with their clients about insurance issues only.

It had been rumored around town that the Boyntons' friends were fearful for their lives. Instead of the usual smile and hello from their friends out on the street, there would be a cool and quick "hi" or they would even pretend that they didn't really see the Boyntons when they passed by them. "My husband and I would say to each other that we were living for the day when African Americans would feel free enough not to get nervous in the presence of a white man," Amelia said.

The Boyntons would receive encouragement to continue with the plight of Blacks through outsiders who came to Selma to work, but were unafraid to lose their jobs, positions or credit with creditors. The Boyntons also found that African Americans living in the country had more determination to be free than Blacks who lived in the cities.

CHAPTER 12
HARASSMENT

It's important that young people know about the struggles we faced to get to the point we are today. Only then will they appreciate the hard-won freedom of blacks in this country.

—AMELIA BOYNTON ROBINSON

The case involved a white woman named Mrs. Hancock, who had told local police authorities that a black man named James Smitherman made a pass at her. Smitherman had a store to which Mrs. Hancock would deliver milk daily.

They would often engage in small talk during her daily rounds. One day, the conversation would be about how her business was booming and profiting—and Mr. Smitherman asked how she managed to get it done. She began to tell him how when one thing led to the next and somehow he ended up giving his phone number to her on a piece of paper. She told the police officers at the station that he was harassing her and she showed them his phone number as proof. She made a call to Mr. Smitherman from the station and policemen listened in on the extension line. Mrs. Hancock would answer the question he asked about her business hoping to lure him into saying something that would prove sexual harassment. He never did. But this wouldn't stop some of the policemen from pursuing the case and arresting him on charges of sexual harassment.

Amelia remembers the story as it was told to her: One evening, a carload of white men wearing hoods rode slowly through the black community in Selma several times. They kidnapped a black man and drove him fifteen miles into the country. The black man finally convinced the Klansmen that he was not Mr. Smitherman. They then left him in the country to walk back to Selma.

Despite Smitherman receiving threatening phone calls about his house being burned down, and threats against his life, he chose to stay in town instead of getting out. So, the following week, Klansmen threw an ignited gallon can of gasoline into a house, thinking that it was his. As it turned out, it was the next-door neighbor's house that was fire bombed. In *Bridge Across Jordan*, Amelia provides vivid details about how the next week bullets were fired into Smitherman's home with evidence pointing to police officers this time. Newspaper articles covered these incidents leading to one of the officers committing suicide.[36]

Still, Smitherman continued to receive threatening phone calls. Some delivery trucks stopped supplying products for his business and Smitherman would eventually close it and leave the city to establish his residence somewhere else.

---

[36] Ibid., 172-173.

Random incidents like the Smitherman case would occur quite often in Selma during the Jim Crow era. Some would be exposed, while other black racial profiling cases would be swept under the table as if they had never happened.

In the spring of 1954, a white woman accused a black man of raping her. She could give no accurate description to the police officers when they arrived. All she knew was that it was a black man. After this, a wave of alleged rape cases appeared across the city, according to Amelia in *Bridge Across Jordan*. Officers could never find a man who could be identified and accused. So, a curfew was declared, but for black men only.

Subsequently, a black man named William Earl Fikes was passing through town one night. Fikes could not read well and didn't know a curfew was in place for all black men in Selma to be off the streets by a certain time. Fikes lived a town over from Selma and had run out of gas between the black and white communities. He, himself, worked for a filling station as an attendant and he started walking down the street looking for the nearest gas station.

Officers spotted him and he became a target because of the curfew. He soon realized someone was following him and so he began to run. As it turns out, the one behind him was a white man, who caught and collared him. When the police arranged for a lineup to identify the black man accused of the latest rape in Selma, the only black man in the lineup was Fikes. The white woman, who was not a reputable person in the community, identified Fikes as her attacker.

Fikes was tried in Selma and quickly given a sentence of 99 years. It was then that Bill determined to do something about it. The Boyntons claimed that it was impossible for this one man to have gone from one side of the city to other, molesting five to ten women in three or four nights. Bill did not believe this, and he felt no one else did. The Boyntons concluded Fikes was just a fall guy who was captured to stop the gossip.

Prosecutors saw to it that there were no blacks on the jury and that there were very few witnesses. The white owner of the filling station where Fikes worked testified that at the time of the crime Fikes had not even left town. The other times when he was accused of being in Selma, it was verified that he either had been at home or at work.

Bill went to Birmingham and convinced two black attorneys, Orzell Billingsley and Peter Hall, to take the Fikes case. He also contacted the National Association Advancement Colored People Legal Defense Fund. (NAACP). Black citizens became aware of the situation and began to give money toward helping to free this innocent man.

No one had the hundreds of thousands of dollars necessary to get him out on bond while the case was appealed, so he remained in jail. Fikes was also tried on another charge brought by the daughter of the former mayor, Mr. Rockwell.

The jury in both trials was all White. The defense had tried its best to get blacks on the panel of jurors, but they were afraid to participate for fear of losing their jobs or being harassed by the Ku Klux Klan if they were to lean toward an innocent verdict for the defendant. Bill was given the jury books to determine if there were any African American on the list to judge the case of Fikes, however, there were none.

Mysteriously, the court slipped in the names of three blacks who had not been listed the night before when Bill had turned in the book. This upset the court, and led to the Whites involved being determined to get rid of Bill before he became a troublemaker. A conspiracy formed that was designed to put Bill out of business.

"We followed up this case, and my husband's speaking out determined his own destiny," This would be the beginning of Bill being harassed and threats on his and Amelia's life, with demands for them leave Selma, Amelia revealed.[37] Based on the reactions of the court, the police department, and the mayor, it had become clear that white supremacists intended to run Bill and Amelia Boynton out of the city of Selma, and, in fact, the state of Alabama.

Meanwhile, the Rockwell-Fikes trial proceeded. The testimonies were inconsistent, weak, and rigged, and consequently, Fikes received the death penalty. Fortunately, on an appeal to the U.S. Supreme Court, the death sentence was thrown out for lack of evidence. Fikes was freed after spending thirteen years in prison for a crime he had never committed. Unbelievable.

Even today, data from across America shows that African American males continue to be labeled and imprisoned with higher sentences for crimes, including rape, burglary, and drug trafficking just because of the black color of their skin.

The examples given above represent unjustified police violence against black people. The blackballing of Bill was later exposed as being corrupt,

---

[37] Ibid., 174.

and was connected with his name appearing on the front page of the newspaper concerning the Fikes case. The article revealed what he had said in court when he acknowledged that he was the one had who brought those black lawyers into Selma.

CHAPTER 13
DISENFRANCHISEMENT

Not all of the U.S.A. is like Selma and Dallas County. All white people are not like the judges and juries I have known. There are peculiar tilts to the law that fit this town with its perpetual board of education and there are customs, manners, and methods that would be strange to any other town in a democratic society.

—AMELIA BOYNTON ROBINSON

In the 1930s there were many beatings, killings, and other cruelties carried out against Blacks, and no one dared say anything. They were afraid that their lives would be in jeopardy. There would be lynchings in Selma area and around the Dallas County areas where "unsung heroes" would be buried in woody areas with unmarked graves. Only the heavens could speak concerning the number of slaves, both bound and free, who were killed and thrown into the Alabama River. It is believed that their souls still wander about seeking revenge for the injustices that resulted in their demise. Amelia saw that the following two decades would be no better as she accurately described in her memoir *Bridge Across Jordan*. Amelia wrote: "I've heard so many sad stories that I began to hate, then pity, then finally I wanted to do something to help these poor, miserable white creatures who were such cowards in, that the only way they could feel important was to 'kill themselves a nigger' or take part in some sort of mob violence."[38]

"De jure and de facto segregation" would rule the Black Belt during the Great Depression until 1965. Although the Emancipation Proclamation had set Negros free, Selma would continue to jail its citizens of color. Then they would work them all day on the streets with a white, pistol-carrying overseer, his hand on the trigger, ready to shoot the first Nigger who got out of line.

When jailed, Blacks were treated like prisoners often were on the *Andy Griffith Show*. Incarcerated citizens of color would find the jail door open in the evening and on weekends to let them go home for meals and so they would have a bed to sleep in. This way the prisoners wouldn't be a financial burden on the city.

Whites police officers usually failed to find any reason to do anything with black educators or businesspeople, who would come to the city to visit relatives or friends. Nevertheless, they were frequently victims of harassment as they were charged with disturbing the peace and would not be discharged until they had paid room and board for their time in jail. "Such things and many more like these incidents had happened in Dallas County," Amelia notes in *Bridge Across Jordan*.

Yes, de jure (or legalized) segregation of Blacks and Whites was present

---

[38] Ibid., 119.

in almost every aspect of life in the South during the Jim Crow era: from public transportation to cemeteries, from prisons to health care, from residences to libraries.[39]

Blacks in this southern region were complacent and from Amelia's first day in Selma, she saw the fear and distrust that hung over Dallas County. Like many others who were brought up in other parts of the country, Amelia had wondered if blacks in this region were content with the life they lived. "I have heard of so many atrocities here in Dallas County that would take thousands of pages to list them," Amelia reminiscences.[40]

One of these atrocities would occur one cool spring night when three black men would come knocking on the Boyntons' back door. She recognized two of the three boys, but wasn't expecting to get an ear full of the mistreatment that these black men had encountered. The oldest of them pleaded with Bill and Amelia not to let the white folks know what they were about to tell them.

The Boyntons reassured them that they would maintain their confidence. As Amelia remembers with a look of astonishment that the eldest recounted, "Jimmy and us [sic] bury [sic] John Henry and he wasn't dead. The Boyntons pondered how they could keep the three black men safe so they could expose the white perpetrators who had done this. They had known John Henry well from the many years of him attending community farmers' club meetings. She felt that he was a smart, quiet, and

---

[39] "What are De jure and De Facto Segregation?" https://www.theedadvocate.org/edupedia/content/what-are-de-jure-and-de-facto-segregation
[40] Ibid., 119.

a righteous man. He was a frank and straight-talking family man who thought that he could hold his own and could manage his own farm. John Henry would be buried alive with his eyes open by the three black men.

In her book, *One Person, No Vote,* by Carol Anderson detailed one example of disenfranchisement when she wrote about rollbacks to African American participation in the vote resulting from the 2013 Supreme Court Decision that eviscerated the Voting Act of 1965. Known as the *Shelby* Ruling, this decision effectively allowed districts with a demonstratable history of racial discrimination to change voting requirements without approval from the Department of Justice.

Chapter 14
THE BOYNTONS MEET MLK, 1954

Long will we remember that great nonviolent leader Martin Luther King, Jr., the man who taught nonviolence to the Western world.

—Amelia Boynton Robinson

It was the summer of 1954 when Bill and Amelia would meet the Reverend Dr. Martin Luther King Jr., and his wife Coretta Scott King at the Dexter Avenue Baptist Church in Montgomery, Alabama. At the time, King had been recently elected as the new pastor. However, he would not make his entrance into Selma until January of 1965.

Dr. King first made headline news around the country due to the Rosa Parks incident, which had ignited the Montgomery bus boycott. Prior to this incident, days, weeks, months and years would go by when men and women were arrested on the buses for even the least resistance to the system—and nothing was done about it.

However, on a cold evening—December 1, 1955 to be exact, Rosa Parks boarded a bus in Montgomery, Alabama and sat down, tired from a long day at work. After the bus was fully loaded with passengers, the white bus driver noticed a white man standing. So, he came to the middle of the aisle where Rosa Parks was sitting and demanded that she get up and give her seat to the white man. She refused. Consequently, the nonviolence fight against injustice began.

News traveled around town fast since Rosa Parks had made the evening broadcast of a special report alerting viewers that a black woman had been arrested for refusing to give up her seat so a white man could sit down.

Dr. King, who was still very much new in the community, and had been busy acclimating himself as the new pastor of the church. Montgomery's most educated and sophisticated black people were members there. The reader needs to keep in mind that Dr. King was not a self-made leader, so when he was chosen to lead the Montgomery bus boycott, there was one key source he could call on first for guidance—God. In *Bridge Across Jordan*, Amelia tells that it wouldn't be until 1985 when she really learnt the truth behind Dr. King being selected to oversee the bus boycott.

It was the afternoon of a bright summer day when E.D. Nixon, a veteran civil rights fighter in Alabama, met Amelia by chance at a doctor's office in Selma. After greeting each other and exchanging some small talk about their health, the dialog drifted to the Rosa Parks incident and the subsequent bus boycott. Nixon let Amelia in on something of which she was not aware.

There had been others arrested for the same reason as Rosa Parks, but this time, all those involved in getting her out of jail felt that it was time to make a move. Rosa made a phone call from jail and explained that she had been arrested. Ed had just gotten off work from the railroad and just finished eating dinner. All the ministers that could come to mind were reached out too. A white attorney named Clifford Durr got her out of jail.

Amelia proceeds to tell the story as she recalls Nixon saying that Joan Robinson, a civil rights activist, began to go into action. Still waiting in the doctor's office for their turn to be called by the nurse, Nixon informed Amelia that on the Monday night after Rosa's trial a meeting was held at Holt Street Baptist church where a name was chosen to name the movement the "Montgomery Improvement Association."

With good reason, Amelia asked how MIA picked a president since there were so many "heavyweight" ministers in Montgomery at the time. Nixon sighed, "Well Amelia, during the confusion and talking about who is to be what, one of the laymen from the floor said, 'I nominate Mr. Ed Nixon as president.'"[41]

Amelia reflects and remembers what Nixon said next: "He never stopped calling me 'Ms. Boynton' and I was too old to be in the confusion, so I said, 'Gentlemen, I'm too old and you've got so many young people who can lead. I decline in favor of this new young preacher, Reverend Martin King.'"[42] Without any hesitation the vote was carried without even questioning what Nixon had proposed, she added. To say the least, Nixon's feelings were hurt because he was passed over and ignored, as they never even asked him if he was sure about not wanting to be the leader for MIA.

Thus, MIA proved to have strong supporters like Reverend Ralph D.

---

[41] Ibid., 202.
[42] Ibid.

Abernathy, Ed Nixon, Robert Nesbitt, Johnnie Carr, and many others who worked and served the organization well, According to Amelia Boynton. MIA would soon serve as an extension to the Southern Christian Leadership Conference (SCLC) where Amelia would serve as second state secretary of a soon to be nationally known organization.

CHAPTER 15
THE CRY OUT, NONVIOLENCE ACTION

Selma feared me because I was going against the racist system.

—AMELIA BOYNTON ROBINSON

Long before the movement in Selma, Alabama in the 1960s, the fight against segregation began many years before. And a century after the American Civil War ended slavery, Jim Crow laws prove to haunt cities across the South with its malicious segregation and discrimination practices against African Americans in these areas: education, housing transportation, jobs, and the right to vote. Amelia notes that African Americans began to awaken and fight for equal rights in the 1950s, once they realized that the U.S. Constitution entitled them to civil rights and voting right privileges as citizens. Selma would soon be the stage for the climax of the struggle to extend civil rights and the right to vote to all Americans, including black people.

Amelia pitied the Blacks in Selma even more because they feared white people would kill them if they were to rise up against them. She was just fed up with seeing all the colored-only and white-only signs around the city. Black-only and white-only drinking fountains, as well as segregated restaurants and hotels across the country, especially in the South, would lead her to finally saying enough is enough. The lynchings, the unsolved murders of blacks who were found floating down the Alabama river, the rapes and the share-cropping of families in the city of Selma and surrounding Dallas County made her and thousands of others realize that the government was far too slow ensuring justice for all its citizens. "Unless we cry out with a loud voice with demonstrations and other agitation, we will always remain in this condition," Amelia Boynton protested.[43]

Alabama State Senator Hank Sanders pointed out: "Today, in the twenty-first century, we should know that the Selma Voting Rights Movement started long before 1965. In fact, Amelia Boynton and husband, Samuel Boynton, initiated efforts to get Blacks to register and vote as far back as the 1930s."[44]

The Dallas County Voters League (DCVL) was a local organization based in the city of Selma that sought to register black voters during the late 1950s and early 1960s.[45] The organization was founded in the 1920s by Charles J. Adams, a postal service employee and civil rights organizer. The DCVL was later revived by an eight-member steering committee known as the "Courageous Eight" made up of Amelia Boynton, Ulysses S. Blackmon, James E. Gildersleeve, Frederick D. Reese, Rev. John D.

---

[43] Ibid., 208.
[44] Hank Sanders. "Courageous Eight have marched final march," Selma Times Journal.com, May 2, 2018, https:// w ww.selmatimesjournal.com/author/hanksander/(accessed July 2019).
[45] "DallasCountyVotersLeague." https://en.wikipedia.org/wiki/Dallas_County_Voters_League

Hunter, Rev. Henry Shannon, Earnest Doyle, and Marie Foster.[46]

The group launched its campaign to register black voters in 1963. Amelia said that the DCVL had been formed to survey what percentage of Blacks were patronizing certain stores in Selma. The DCVL committee became aware that some stores were patronized by a majority of Blacks, who were only being hired for unskilled jobs like cooking, housekeeping and cleaning bathrooms. Many obstacles were put in place to discourage the organization from trying to desegregate, and change how local stores were operating and treating Blacks, Amelia admitted.

Storeowners in Selma ranted with rage that no Niggers would be hired for positions of significance like running the cash register or being salesmen. In fact, most stores she visited let it be known that the White Citizens' Council had sent a committee around to the stores to fire the Niggers they had working for them. Most even went so far as to tell the committee that before they would employ another Nigger or let the committee dictate to them how to run their business, they would close their doors to all the Niggers, Amelia added.

Those on the committee didn't lose their tempers because they knew how racist white people were in Selma. A few days after this, a mass meeting was called to vote on a boycott of all white stores as soon as the Christmas rush had started. The black community held onto their money and told their children that there would be no Santa Claus that year.

Amelia noted that the merchants began to feel the pinch and so the

---

[46] Ibid.

merchants demanded a meeting with the committee, begging them to stop the boycott. The boycott was so successful that it was decided that this would be the most effective way to demand respect, Amelia admitted.

Selma was so accustomed to Blacks being mistreated that they didn't understand why the Niggers had turned away and resented being treated like animals. A meeting was held with the white people in order to come to some agreement that all could live with. According to Amelia, several meetings were held, but no agreement could be reached for Blacks to have equal status with Whites. "We were citizens of America and of Selma, and we paid our taxes like everyone else in the city. We felt it was our duty, to get as much as anyone else and to demand respect also," Amelia recalled.

Several days later, a meeting was called to meet with the mayor's office, but Amelia's committee was not invited. Instead, the mayor's office had picked other black citizens to attend the meeting. Once there, they were told what they could expect that there was no intention of giving black citizens in Selma their freedom. Amelia noted that "Those called to the meeting were the Reverend C.C. Brown, Calvin Osborne, Dr. Sullivan Jackson, and Warner Reid."

The black committee had planned that when these meetings were almost over the original committee members would walk in and surprise the "White Supremacy" powers. They made clear that African Americans were unified in their fight against segregation in the city of Selma and they would continue until every sign of discriminatory practices would be done away with there and throughout the country.

In 1965, DCVL worked with the Student Nonviolent Coordinating

Committee (SNCC) and the Southern Christian Leadership Conference (SCLC) to organize the Selma-to-Montgomery marches. Although the Civil rights Act of 1964 was passed to legally end the practice of segregation, Amelia and the DCVL found it difficult to any black voters registered. In the winter of 1964, they would receive the help of the SCLC. The SCLC would be led by the Reverend Dr. Martin Luther King Jr. and this would all set the stage for the 1965 Selma Voting Rights Campaign on January 2, 1965.[47]

---

[47] Ibid.

Chapter 16
AMELIA, 1ST NEGRO WOMAN FOR CONGRESS

The article identified me as the first female member of her race ever to seek a seat in Congress from Alabama. I was also the first woman, white or black, to run on the Democratic ticket.

—Amelia Boynton Robinson

It was the spring of 1954—five years before Dallas County's civil rights struggle was known to the world. Bill and Amelia had been there before the Civil Rights Commission in Montgomery, Alabama, telling of the horrific murders, lynchings, rapes, and brainwashing of African Americans living in the city of Selma and the rural areas of Dallas County, Alabama.

Amelia and Bill emotionally and vividly described for the CRC the atrocities that black folks were experiencing in Selma. Some had been forced off the plantation because they tried to register to vote. Others were beaten because they had gone to voter clinics that Bill had held in the counties. And how many blacks had lost their jobs for attempting to register to vote? Amelia went on to describe the scare tactics that were used by officers of the law to intimidate people into not going to the meeting places.

Amelia remembers that she and Bill were praised for their courage to come forward with this information. However, CRC feared the worst because of the exposure given to the atrocities in Selma. So, it was advised by CRC to take the backroads as they returned to Selma. Everyone knew that certain backroads had to be avoided after dark because of the fear of being caught and lynched by the Ku Klux Klan, she notes. Let's put it like this: You had to get back to Selma before the sunset.

Getting black folks into Selma in those days wasn't as easy a task. It would be six years before mass meetings in the county or city would be held, Amelia said. Black people would come from counties around to hear how they could win their freedom. She notes that it was a beautiful sight to see. Most ministers in Selma had to be begged to open their churches for voter registration meetings. Amelia remembered: The armory schools, court houses and other political places were off limits. In fear for their lives due to opening their doors for mass meetings related to voting rights, ministers would conveniently disappear at meeting time, according to Mrs. Boynton.

During these trying times of getting the Selma and Dallas County African American to vote, Amelia was often greeted on the streets of Selma with sneers and jeers. Even after arriving home late at night from the mass voting meeting, her neighbors would often greet her the same way for being a troublemaker in the community. Black people were always talking about the Boyntons being troublemakers and stirring up stuff with the white people in town.

Some did not want change and desired for the situation to remain like it was, Amelia explained. For weeks, Amelia and Bill continued to receive anonymous threatening phone calls with cursing and threats of bombing their home if they didn't stop the voter registration movement.

Even during the Fikes trial that was mentioned in a prior chapter, the phone rang one morning about 3 o'clock. Amelia recalled in anguish that when she answered the phone she heard a heavy voice say, "Nigger, we ain't gonna have you all trying to change things around here. Git out of town and damn quick."

All these threats would make Amelia even more determined to fight for what she knew was right. She was tough and had made up her mind that no one would run them out of their home, even with the threats of bombing. There were always many friends who stood guard around their home and they gave the Boyntons the strength to continue. Several weeks passed before the Boyntons could rest at night without getting phone calls from people threatening kill them.

Amelia said it was her faith in God that she depended on for guidance. She felt He had groomed her for this struggle—the struggle included the white man, and many came to help from across the country.

Bill told Amelia that he thought someday she might run for U.S. Congress. She chuckled, finding it awkward that he would make a statement like this. Bill continued by saying that was not at all far-fetched to believe that one day African Americans would be registered voters in the South without repercussions.

The anxiety of trying to get black folks in Selma to come out to registration meetings became a strain on Bill's health. And the stress of being killed by a white person in town weighed heavily on his heart and mind. Bill ended up having a stroke amidst all of this commotion.

Amelia explains that he had a stroke and became paralyzed, and so was confined to a wheelchair until the end of his life. On the occasions when Bill went to the hospital, he would still talk to anyone passing by his doorway—reminding them to register and vote.

Bill died on May 13, 1963 and his death stirred up a lot of black people in the community. Perhaps because of guilt, they decided to have the first mass meeting the night of his death in Selma.

After Bill's passing, Amelia became more involved with fighting for human rights. The following year she spoke at Tuskegee Institute at a regional meeting of the Women's International League for Peace and Freedom.

She told them about Selma: the Black Belt, the struggle, and the African Americans who wanted freedom. "My husband's words came back to me and at the end of my talk, I heard myself saying that I might run for Congress this year from my district," she visualized. This would be the first time that Amelia had taken the idea seriously.

No plans or platform had been laid out. It was the eleventh hour for candidates in the race. And Amelia knew that if she wanted to be on the ballot, a decision had to be made right away. After her speech, the audience cheered her on to run.

Impressed with the organization's fight against the war, poverty, and civil rights, when the opportunity came around, she joined. The integrated group would eventually open a branch in Selma where they focused on a door-to-door campaign for voter registration, a variety of food banks, and clothing drives to help the needy. They used the Laubach method of teaching so that the community could learn how to read and write. They also persuaded a local white minister to take part in the human rights effort in order to move the city of Selma in the right direction.

Amelia was rallying local Selma citizens to register and vote. She also worked with the Women's International League in helping the homeless, poor, and needy. At the same time, she put her name on the ballot to run for Congress.

"I'm going to win," Selma businesswoman Amelia Boynton told The Washington Post by phone.[48] If she would win, she would become the first Negro Representative from Alabama since Reconstruction days. The population of Dallas County, of which Selma is the seat, was more than 50 percent Negro. Yet fewer than two percent of the Negroes who were of voting age were registered.

In 1964, she would receive 11 percent of the primary vote. This made her the first woman, white or black to have the Democratic nomination in Alabama. A key point that Boynton made throughout her travels and speeches throughout the country was that her run for the congress seat encouraged other blacks to register and vote.

In 1974, Boynton would again put her hat in the ring, but this time it would be for the State Senate. She would not win, but her run would

---

[48] "Mississippi Freedom Democratic Party records." Historical Society Library Microf 1/1 (1963-1965): http://content.wisconsinhistory.org/cdm/ref/collection/p15932c0 1112/id/37808

encourage other blacks to register and vote—which was part of her mission in life.

CHAPTER 17
VOTER SUPPRESSION

And we would tell them: There are two things. You are not independent; you are not a citizen. You're going to have to do things—you're going to have to control some money, and you're going to have to vote. Because a vote-less people is a hopeless people.

—AMELIA BOYNTON ROBINSON

It was in the fall 1962. The leaves on trees, shrubs, and plants began to turn gold, scarlet, and orange. Bernard Lafayette, a student active with SCLC, had arrived in Selma to do a study on living conditions in the black community.

Around Christmas of the same year, his wife Colia joined him to set up a plan that would document through a survey the age, occupation, and number of people living in each African American household in Selma and as well as far beyond the city limits. The plan was put into play by local students—teenage boys and girls. They went from door to door, giving out the survey forms which specifically focused on the number of registered voting living in the home.

Two years passed and voter registration classes were up and operating. Students were meeting up at the home of Margaret J. Moore, a local teacher, where they continued to receive training from Bernard Lafayette, according to Amelia Boynton. Lafayette had been living there so he could stay abreast of the voter's registration drive.

The house was always filled with students—which was suspicious to the city police and the sheriff's department. To stop local blacks from learning how to fill out voter registration forms, the police constantly arrested the boys and girls. As word got around that these students were being mistreated and harassed more and more parents and residents became interested. Amelia noted that the crowds grew larger in support of what was happening to their children. Local churches like First Baptist Church and Tabernacle Baptist Church (ministers M.C. Cleveland J., and L.L. Anderson) opened their doors in order to help assist in the training for voter registration and nonviolence. Reverend Hunter, pastored the AME Zion church on Lawrence Street, which would be the first church in Selma that permitted voter educational training, as Amelia states in *Bridge Across Jordan.*[49]

By the end of 1964, participation had grown to the point that other places were sought out for voter registration training. By now, Governor Wallace had changed the window for applications to every two weeks and made it even harder to pass the voting test. Instead of a two-page form, it was now several pages long, Amelia Boynton stated. Brown Chapel AME Church was chosen to pick up the overflow of people now participating in

---

[49] Ibid., 226.

the voter registration training. The adults were asked to gather at Brown Chapel while the youth remained at First Baptist Church, Ms. Boynton recalled. Additional training was given on self-control and Christian ways of reacting to discrimination, she added.

1964 also saw Sheriff Jim Clark and his deputies patrolling the church meetings with the aim of breaking up the meeting and sending people home in terror.

There was one meeting that Boynton recalled when Sheriff Clark sent the deputies into the church to pick up the leader of the meeting, but the men did not know who that was—so, they left out without him. This angered Clark even more. "He entered the church while the young Reverend Bennie Tucker was on his knees praying. He walked up to the young man, collared him, and dragged him while his deputies cattle-prodded him to the waiting sheriff's car," Amelia explained.[50]

The next day, over 400 adults marched up to the Dallas County Courthouse to register. But the doors were locked and men were posted who were carrying knives and shotguns. All were silenced as they stood outside the courthouse waiting for the building to open. Once the building was open, no one was allowed to step out of line and if they did, Sheriff Jim Clark had declared that their place would be lost: The bathrooms were intentionally locked to force some to leave, because restrooms were all limited for use.

It was a hot, hazy, muggy day with the sun sweltering down on the

---

[50] Ibid., 228.

prospective registrants. The pavement was hard with nowhere to sit, but these black people were determined to hold up like soldiers, hoping that somewhere in his heart, Jim Clark would open the doors for them to go into the courthouse and register.

Nevertheless, at 3:30 in the afternoon, the people got tired of standing from heat exhaustion. "No one would have the opportunity to register," Amelia sighed. There would be many times after this attempt when blacks would line up in the cold, in the rain, or in the hot sun only to be let down, turned away or even jailed.

It was one hot spring day in May of 1964 when James Forman and John Lewis of SNCC and Marie Foster prepared sandwiches and lemonade to serve the people in line waiting. Ms. Boynton commented that this was all to no avail as Sheriff Clark had stood proud saying, "I'll be damn if you do. If you bring water or anything, I will arrest you for molesting." Amelia was dumbfounded by the word "molesting" as she stood there in the sweltering heat in front of the Selma Dallas County Court House, staring Clark straight in the face. "Molesting?!" She shouted. "If giving human beings something to eat when they are hungry is molesting, then mothers molest the babes in the crib!."[51]

This day would be historic for Amelia. And it meant the world to her to see hundreds of people in line to register to vote. Among them were teachers, ministers, professionals, and businessmen and women, as well as domestic workers and housewives.

---

[51] Ibid., 229.

As Amelia began to walk across the street, she heard a white man in the crowd say, "Git 'em!" she recalls in *Bridge Across Jordan*. "What's all the commotion that's going on over there?" Amelia asked the crowd standing in line at the courthouse awaiting their opportunity to go inside and register to vote. Two of the deputies were beating up two black men. They yelled to her across the street where she stood. White people began to run to where the officers were attacking two young black men. The officers handcuffed them and shoved them into a bus. A tall skinny white man among the spectators took it upon himself to walk over to the bus and curse the two black youths loudly, shaking his finger in their faces, Ms. Boynton explained.

The two black men had brought all this on themselves by trying to give a sandwich and a drink of water to an elderly man who had been standing in that long line, eager to take the voting registration test in order to have the privilege to vote. After the white man had finally said everything that was on his mind to the black men on the bus, he walked away lethargically. Later that evening, while discussing with others the beating of the two black boys, Amelia discovered that the white man was Mr. Dunn, co-owner of the Dunn Rest Home.

As it turns out, Mr. Dunn had been slowly walking down the street, searching for any of his employees who might be in those long lines. He spotted two nurses' aides, Elnora Collins and Annie Cooper, who worked for him. Ms. Boynton remembered as plainly as if it was yesterday that when Annie realized that Mr. Dunn had seen them, she told Elnora, who had remarked that they had just lost their jobs. Ms. Cooper was scheduled to be off the next day, but when the secretary of Dunn Rest Home called to inform her that she was fired, Annie was not surprised.

What happened next? That night, 40 more employees of the rest home called for a meeting and asked for Amelia to attend. By a unanimous vote they decided to ask Mr. Dunn for Ms. Cooper's job back, threatening that they would all leave if he didn't agree. According to Ms. Boynton, the petition they drew up included other grievances including the need for a raise in salary (since they were only being paid $16 a week), work hours to be cut from twelve to eight hours a day, and provision for sick leave and insurance. Amelia described the petition as being typed, signed, and sent with one of the nurses who acted as the representative for the group. They decided to give the petition to Mr. Dunn at 10.00 o'clock the next morning.

The work day started earlier, and so everyone was already there, including Elnora. Dunn suspected that something was up because he had seen an unusually large gathering of nurses around the rest home. In the meantime, he sent for Ms. Collins to come to his office. She had been expecting to be fired for trying to register to vote as well.

Amelia recalled that Dunn, angrily said, "Elnora, you're fired. I don't need you around her any longer." Elnora simply smiled and said, "Thank you, Mr. Dunn."[52]

Amelia explained that Dunn's employees usually addressed him as "doctor" to show respect, although he didn't have a medical degree. Elnora left the office knowing in her mind that everything had gone well. Dunn

---

[52] Ibid., 230.

had accepted that she was okay with being fired, but before she could get out to tell the others what had happened, his secretary called her back to say that Mr. Dunn wanted to speak with her again.

As she entered his office, she found him standing in front of his desk with a camera. He ordered her to face him so he could get a good picture. This was the method used by white people to keep African Americans from being hired by anyone else. She held her purse up to her face and said, "I'm not going to let you take my picture, because I know just what you're going to do with it," Amelia reminisced, telling the story just like it was told to her by Elnora.[53]

Frustrated and angry at this point. Dunn put down the camera and picked up a cattle prod that he had used on one of the janitors. Amelia was aware of what had happened to him because it had been talked about throughout the black community.

Ms. Collins tried to run out of the office, but he caught her and beat her all over the head, across the shoulders and on her back. He shocked her entire body with the cattle prod ,inflicting pain and bruises, Amelia recalled. Elnora ran out of the office, down the stairs and into the street screaming.

All 40 of the nurses left their post and walked out of the rest home in protest. The woman who was supposed to give the petition to Mr. Dunn remembered it just in time to give it to the secretary as she passed her in the hallway. This all happened early in the morning about 7:30 a.m. "I

---

[53] Ibid., 230.

knew all of this because there were 40 nurses who came to my house to tell me what happened. My first instinct was to take Ms. Collins to a doctor and have the entire group go with us,"[54] Amelia offered. Well, everyone did go. And Ms. Collins was treated for burns and bruises. The Justice Department and the FBI were contacted, and many sworn statements were taken by them, she noted.

Did anything happen to the administrators at Dunn Rest Home? Amelia noted that the same thing that happened to all white people who mistreated African Americans. Nothing, except for a pat on the back from other racists.

As Amelia recalled, by late 1967, Mr. Dunn had passed to his reward and the Dunn Rest Home had become integrated. Folks in the Selma community said Mr. Dunn often would tell the white people that he just couldn't take it. He couldn't accept those Niggers getting their freedom and all the changes that desegregation had caused. Most said he got sick and died with a broken heart. White Selma blacklisted these women, making it hard for them to find jobs. Annie Lee Cooper finally found a job at the black-owned Torch Motel, according to a report from the *Digital SNCC Gateway.*[55]

---

[54] Ibid., 230.

[55] "Annie Lee Cooper" https://snccdigital.org/people/annie-lee-cooper/

CHAPTER 18
THE JIM CROW SOUTH

For 30 Years, we fought to get such a small number of people registered! And how we did it, I don't know. We had to do it, through some of the white people who wanted somebody to vote for them.

—AMELIA BOYNTON ROBINSON

During winter, when temperatures were around 32 degrees in the city of Selma, the New Year had come and gone. Most of the youngsters around town had no Thanksgiving or Christmas worth much in the prior year. The reason for this was that their parents had been fired by the white supremacists in the city who wished that the Niggers would stay in their places and stop causing trouble.

And if truth be told, most Blacks in Selma wanted no changes. They had become content with working on the plantations as sharecroppers and didn't want to cause "Mr. Massa" any problems. And yet, Amelia saw that some of the people staying on the farms began to see their lives were hopeless and wanted change. They were more open to help, too, Amelia felt, because she and her husband had been working with the people in the rural areas for over 30 years—teaching them how to farm, read, write, count money, become landowners, and go through voter registration.

By the spring of 1963, over 600 Blacks were out of jobs. The reason? They were fired because of their participation in some stages of the civil rights movements. No one would hire them, and many had families at home to feed.

This led to critical problems in the Selma community. Many had bills that were overdue, and eviction notices had been issued. SNCC sent out a request around the country soliciting help from anyone who would provide financial help to the Selma movement. There was a domino effect on other areas across the Black Belt as other cities and counties attempted to register voters as Ms. Boynton recounted.

SNCC's plea was heard. Food, medicine, clothing, and other supplies began to come in by the truckloads. Amelia was happy to see all that the Blacks, both low and middle class, started coming together for the movement. However, the black ministers and deacons of local churches were still uncommitted out of fear for their lives from the Whites in the city.

Amelia Boynton describes tears flowing down her face as she felt, and they believed that freedom was coming soon. But she realized that her strength came from God and that this was not a time for crying. She raised her head up and started to remember what her husband Bill had told her as he lay in the hospital bed suffering from three strokes and a heart attack: "Continue the fight in getting the people the right to vote."

Immediately, Amelia made phone calls to the Employment Bureau of

Alabama, informing them that their employment agency was referring some women for employment. But, as expected, nothing happened as a result of the plea. The women were simply brushed off by the white establishment as they emphasized that no work was available at the time. If something did come open, the women were told that they had to be high school graduates. And even when they presented a high school diploma, they were simply given a card to hold onto until something became available. The women never received a call.

Something had to be done. But what?

Amelia came up with a master plan. She and her friend Marie Foster brought together a number of ideas about how to get the people to work. The team consisted of several notable women in Selma, including Mrs. Ruth Lindsey, Mrs. Geneva Martin, Miss Idell Rawls, Mrs. Foster, Mrs. Gloria Maddox.

They determined that the project would be set into motion by the Dallas County Voter League and the vote was unanimous: Amelia Boynton would speak on the team's behalf at DCVL. This made sense since Amelia was already familiar with the project because her sister, Elizabeth Smith, who lived in Philadelphia, had operated a small clothing factory for over 30 years.

The First Baptist Church minister, the Reverend M. C. Cleveland, offered the church basement to train the women how to sew clothes using the sewing machine. The Reverend Ralph Smeltzer of the Church of the Brethren made the contacts for work contracts. He also made the connections for Mrs. Martin and Miss Rawls to go to Maryland for training courses that would teach them how to train the others. Other white friends sent sewing machines and the applications for work came in by the hundreds from people who wanted to work. White people began to complain to the sheriff, which led to him block gatherings at the church for the training sessions.

Besides being responsible for the complex voting application (that even he couldn't pass), Governor Georg Wallace put forth another effort to take his Jim Crow laws north. As a result, an organization was formed in Baltimore in order to stop the good governor of Alabama from infecting their city with these racist tactics. GROW (Get Rid of Wallace) was created to let the nation know about the principles the man stood for, Amelia explained. GROW sent a letter asking her to come to Baltimore to challenge Wallace and his campaign of hate.

Five rallies were held in Baltimore on Sunday May 10, 1964 and Amelia Boynton spoke at all of them, and then later at John Hopkins University. There she found that the students and faculty were in sympathy with the blacks of Dallas County. Amelia described the mood of the audiences she had spoken to on that day as showing pity for all the black folks down south who had been enduring this harsh treatment for so long. They thought that something had to be done to stop this man before other "little Wallaces" and "little Hitlers" began to sprout up all over the country.

Upon returning home, Amelia received an injunction from Sheriff Jim Clark to stop the training meeting at the church. The letter specified that African Americans were not to come together at any time whatsoever. There were to be no more walk-ins, sit-ins, or any other form of demonstration.

Amelia Boynton took the letter to the SNCC and they all read it together. The letter specifically named Martin Luther King Jr, James Bevel, Amelia Boynton, Marie Foster, L.L. Anderson and many more. The injunction included all the ministers of local African American churches as well as some in the rest of the country.

After hearing about the injunction, older African Americans started going to the registrar's office, but all failed to pass the test each time it was given. Educators, business and professional people all took an oral examination from a white person who had no more than an eighth-grade education himself (but with perhaps the advantage of being rich).

Ms. Boynton added that she had been told by a white friend that she had been given a book of questions to study to prepare for registration. Amelia soon discovered that whites visited the courthouse on a different schedule—after hours. She further noted that many whites didn't even need to register at all because they had been voters for years already.

All these trickeries are what led to the historic 50-mile march from Selma to Montgomery on March 21, 1965. Much blood would be shed in the lead-up to the march to the Alabama Capital for the right to vote as black citizens in America.

CHAPTER 19
BATTLE FOR FREEDOM

Sheriff Jim Clark looked at me as I'm walking down the street: C'mon here and get in this line! I said I'm going to my office! He ran behind me and grabbed me by the nape of my neck, turned me around and started pushing me toward the paddy wagon. And I said, I hope the news media gets this. Clark said, I hope so too!

—AMELIA BOYNTON ROBINSON

Several decades had now passed. And the Boyntons had become a household name around the city of Selma. Amelia would continue to run the real estate and employment agency business that she and her husband Samuel "Bill" Boynton had been operating for over 30 years. Amelia dearly missed Bill, but she remembered what he told her on his deathbed: "Amelia, don't let these people down. See to it that they all have the right to vote. Don't give up the fight."

There was much screaming, crying and agony going on at the jail house for many years. And since the office was located across the street from the Selma jail, she often heard the men and women screaming from the sound of belts beating their stark-naked backs.

"Injustice to say to least!" she exclaimed. Out of all the beatings, kicking, and clubbing without mercy, black folks seem to forgive and forget without hate in their hearts. But Amelia saw it differently. She saw it as fear and ignorance on the part of African Americans.

The people in Selma were sick and tired of being sick and tired of this continual denial of civil and human rights. The same was felt by other African Americans across the state of Alabama and throughout the country. Amelia noticed that the people whom she and Bill had been teaching in the rural districts were the ones who were hungry to become citizens. "We had our office downtown in Selma, and of course, the county is 772 square miles, which means we had quite a large area,"[56] Amelia Boynton stated.

But all these incidents with Sheriff Jim Clark and white citizens isn't what ignited the decision to march to Montgomery. As Amelia vividly remembered, it started in Marion, in Perry County, which was the next county over from Selma. In an interview with the *Executive Intelligence Review*, Mrs. Boynton recalled that the black people in Marion were having mass meetings just like the ones being held in Selma.[57] They were at a church, she added. And after the meeting, some of the people went to a black drugstore. A state trooper came into the drug store and for some reason started beating a woman who was in a wheelchair. So, her son, Jimmy Lee Jackson, tried to protect his mother from the beating. In retaliation, trooper shot him in the back, and he died a few days later at

---

[56] Notley.
[57] Ibid.

the Good Samaritan Hospital in Selma. After his death, SCLC and the black people declared, "We're going to take the casket to Montgomery, and put it on the steps of the capitol,"[58] Amelia Boynton conveyed. But instead of taking the casket to Montgomery, which was 80 miles away, it was decided that a march from Selma to Montgomery was needed to plead the cause for voting rights.

In the meantime, Amelia went out of the courthouse through the side door. And there was Jim Clark standing in front of the building, keeping people from going into the courthouse. These were older people, many of whom had lost their jobs because they went to Bill's memorial service when he died. Many were old with canes, but they were determined to register to vote.

When Clark saw Amelia walking down the street, he demanded, "Where are you going?" Amelia told the sheriff that she was going back to her office and then he yelled, "Oh no you are not!"[59] Sheriff Clark then proceeded to grab Amelia by the coat and push her around and started to shove her down the street back to the courthouse. Amelia was stunned to see all the cameramen and newspaper reporters around and knowing how Clark liked publicity, she told him that she hoped the reporters would see how he had her coat collar tangled around her neck as he continued to shove her toward the court house.

What was his Sheriff Clark's reaction? "He said, 'Dammit, I hope they do,'"[60] Mrs. Boynton described.

---

[58] Notley.
[59] Ibid., 245.
[60] Ibid., 246.

The African Americans who continued to wait in the long registration line that curved around the corner of the courthouse into a cold narrow alleyway watched indignantly. Amelia didn't know what to think. All this was happening too fast. She felt alone. But after she heard them protesting her going jail, Mrs. Boynton heard them say that they were going to jail, too.

What more consolation would a person need? And with another push, the sheriff shoved her into a deputy's car and said, "Arrest this woman and put her in jail." Upon arrival to the Selma Police Department, Amelia's purse was searched and taken away. She was fingerprinted five times and given a card with a number so her picture could be taken. She was booked on charges of criminal provocation, namely inciting Blacks to be good citizens and that was crime enough.

Amelia remembered the episode as if it were yesterday. She recalled being brutally handled, pushed down the hallway, and thrown in a jail cell to await her judgment by white supremacists. She had cried as she thought about the outcome of all that she had experienced.

But later that evening, she heard the group who had cheered her on at the courthouse. *Who else could it be?* she asked herself. They were singing the newly born civil rights song: "Oh freedom, oh freedom, oh freedom over me. And before I'll be a slave, I'll be buried in my grave, and go home to my Lord and be free."[61] It was so sweet and yet so sad to hear, Amelia mourned, as she remembered what it was like when the cell door slammed shut.

---

[61] Ibid., 246.

Night came and a group of about 60 African Americans supporters, some of them local school teachers who had come to support Mrs. Boynton, were charged with unlawful assembly and released. Amelia Boynton would be the last one to be released on criminal provocation with her bond being set higher than the others. The next day, Mrs. Boynton went to Birmingham and met with her attorney to file a court order against Sheriff Clark. This would set aside his order against unlawful assembly of African Americans in Dallas County.

Amelia told her attorney to be quick about all he had to do because she had to get back to Selma by 2:30 in the afternoon. It was Friday, January 22, and the teachers were going to march to the courthouse. The teachers were in fear of losing their jobs because of the arrest, so they voted to call all the teachers to demonstrate as a group against the brutal treatment and the mass arrests.

The lawyers laughed and said Mrs. Boynton stopped wasting time thinking that the teachers were going to stick together. Amelia arrived back in time to join the teachers who were led in their march by the president of the Dallas County Teachers Association, the Reverend Frederick D. Reese. Amelia smiled and said there were about 135 teachers and only three were absent from the demonstration.

Standing with pride on the steps, staring Sheriff Clark straight in the eye, they announced their plan to go to the registrar's office. The Sheriff stood before the group with his cattle prod and began to push the teachers off the steps, added Mrs. Boynton.

"Go! Gather up your teachers and take 'em back to the school where they came from! You hear me?" Sheriff Clark scoffed.[62]

Rev. Dr. Frederick D. Reese responded: "This courthouse does not belong to you, Sheriff Clark. This courthouse belongs to all of us. And as citizens of this country, we're here to see if the Board of Registrars is in session. We have a right to enter this courthouse, and we will not back down from that right."[63]

The sheriff's threats didn't stop crowd from trying to get through. They kept moving each time the deputies, who hardly had an eighth-grade education, tried to stop them. Mrs. Boynton added that the teachers failed in reaching the registrar's office, but they let the sheriff, the deputies and the other whites know that they were not afraid and that they had joined the battle for freedom.

---

[62] Frederick D. Reese and Kathy M. Walters. Selma's Self-Sacrifice.
[63] Ibid., 1.

CHAPTER 20

EDMUND PETTUS BRIDGE, BLOODY SUNDAY

When we got just a little across the bridge, I saw these state troopers; I saw the sheriff's deputies—some of them were on the Selma side. I saw the police. And the state troopers were in front. And I said to my friend Marie Foster, "My gosh! Those people look like tin soldiers!"

—AMELIA BOYNTON ROBINSON

Many often ask what triggered the march from Selma to Montgomery, Alabama. Some think that it was all the incidents that happened with Sheriff Jim Clark in Selma.

No, that wasn't it, Amelia has explained. It didn't happen in Jim Clark's county, it was in Marion, Perry County, which is the next county over. Amelia explained in an interview on February 18, 2005 with Katherine Notley, a freelance writer for the Executive *Intelligence Review.*[64]

They were having mass meetings for voting rights at a church just like

[64] Notley.

the ones in Selma. After these meetings, some of the protestors went into a black drugstore and for some reason a state trooper went into the store and started beating a woman who was in a wheelchair. And her son made an attempt to protect his mother from being beaten. So, during Jimmy Lee's tussle with the troopers, they shot him twice in the stomach. Days later, he passed away in the Good Samaritan Hospital in Selma. It was later reported in official government records that the criminal who was called out to search for an atrocious crime was Alabama State Trooper James Fowler.

After all this happened, the communities of Marion and Selma, as well as the SCLC agreed this needed be made known at the state capital so Governor George C. Wallace would know what had happened. By unanimous vote, the casket would be taken to Montgomery and placed on the steps of the capitol building. However, as Mrs. Boynton pointed out, instead of taking the casket to Montgomery, the decision was made to march from Selma to Montgomery in order to plead the case.

Rev. Frederick D. Reese was the president of the Dallas County Voters League at this time. The majority of DCVL members were school teachers working in the Selma city school system with the exception of Amelia Boynton who was a self-employed local businesswoman. Because of Judge Hare's injunction against the blacks in the city, Rev. Reese's colleagues had agreed that a secret committee needed to be created to get around it. So, a group of Selma's prominent leaders came together to discuss these issues and concerns, and develop strategies in order to advance the voting rights movement.

"The Courageous Eight," as they were nicknamed, came together in reaction to the injunction to control blacks in Selma. They determined that the injunction gave legal legitimacy to ongoing disenfranchisement and unjust treatment of African Americans.

The Courageous Eight members consisted: Amelia Boynton, Rev. Frederick D. Reese, Ulysses Blackmon, Earnest Doyle, Marie Foster, James Edward Gildersleeve, Rev. Henry Shannon and Rev. J. D. Hunter. "I advised my fellow Courageous Eight members that it would be in our best interest to invite Martin Luther King, Jr. to Selma"[65]

So, in late 1964, Boynton sought additional support for her struggles in Selma. According to Andrew Young, it was Mrs. Boynton who approached Dr. King first before Christmas in 1964 and said, 'You need to come and help us in Selma,' and that is where the Selma movement started."[66] She inspired King and members of the SCLC to act in Selma, Young added. Reese would appear to concur with Amelia. So, just before Christmas, in 1964 the Courageous Eight met at Amelia Boynton's home for a discussion concerning the best tactics and strategies press forward with the movement.[67]

Around October 1964, Rev. Martin Luther King Jr. had arrived in Selma to participate in several marches from Brown Chapel Church up to the Dallas courthouse to protest for the right to vote in the registrar's office. Dr. King was arrested by Sheriff Clark and his deputies alongside Rev.

---

[65] Ibid., 114-115.
[66] Kevin R. Johnson, "Women of Selma-to-Montgomery March," ThePhiladelphiaTribune, March 7, 2015. https://w ww.phillytrib.com/commentary/women-of-Selma-to-Montgomery-march/article4_.
[67] Frederick D. Reese and Kathy M. Walters. Selma's Self-Sacrifice.

Fredrick D. Reese, other leaders, and many protestors for marching without a permit through the streets of Selma.

Upon being released from their cells, the marchers would regroup and strategize once again. However, the threats, beatings and terrorization continued to emerge throughout the city causing much fear amongst the ministers, leaders, and blacks in Selma. Judge Hare's injunction to prevent African Americans from gathering under the assumption that they would be to protest civil and voting rights issues, included churches, shopping stores, and eateries. "Martin Luther King Jr. made it known that because of these strict rules ordered in the injunction, he would not return to Selma for participation in future demonstration until given a proper invitation," Rev. Reese revealed. [68]

The injunction caused the momentum to shift by weakening the core of the movement. This had been noticed widely by SCLC, SNCC and The Courageous Eight as the number of protestors had dropped and overall morale was down greatly. Amelia's first thoughts were that the recent arrests and threats and some unsung killings had brought fear into the minds of the citizens in Selma. A lot of progress had been made and no one in the movement wanted this to be a setback as Mrs. Boynton noted.

The group felt that choosing Dr. King to come to Selma would push the movement forward. Dr. King had been proven a leader by being a Nobel prize winner with notoriety all around for his past accomplishments with civil rights. The Courageous Eight also felt that Rev. Martin Luther King was a great orator with incredible charisma who could move local

---

[68] Ibid.

ministers to step up to the plate and encourage their congregations to stand up and fight for their freedom. And King's record spoke for itself.

Reese alludes to the proven fact that he and the SCLC held an impressive record for raising revenue and helped to boost voting campaigns in other cities. As the leader of The Courageous Eight, Reese and all group members signed the written letter to officially invite both Martin Luther King, Jr. and the SCLC to Selma.

On January 17, 1965, SNCC Chairman John Lewis kicked off the voter registration drive at a mass meeting in Selma. Dr. Martin Luther King and his staff arrived on January 18. A 500-strong march on the county courthouse was led by Dr. Martin Luther King and SNCC Chairman John Lewis. They were forced to stand all day in an alley and none of the protesters were able to take the voter's test.

According to Ms. Boynton, Dr. King had registered in the Albert Hotel in Selma, one of the old landmarks, built with slave labor around the 1880s. Boynton described this hotel as being designed to be a replica of the Doge's Palace in Venice.

"The Albert" had a beautiful left wing and a right-winding staircase to either side of an oval mezzanine. But a horrible incident would happen to King while he was there, Amelia explained. Dr. King was kicked and punched by a white man who was led away by his racism in this newly integrated Selma hotel.

By now the new mayor, Joseph "Joe" T. Smitherman, who had only been in office for about a month, continued to receive complaints from white-owned businesses, white racists, and from the white community in general throughout the city of Selma.

They saw Dr. King and the infiltration of the SCLC and SNCC organization as troublemakers and a threat to the white people's way of life and living, Amelia recollects. This thinking was true for most white citizens of Selma and for those blacks who had been brainwashed that their way of living as second class citizens was the right way. Amelia and her husband Bill understood the white people in Selma and some blacks also wished that they had packed their bags up and left the city long ago. They were considered troublemakers. And most blacks in Selma and surrounding rural areas were afraid to speak up for themselves for fear of losing their jobs or being shot and found dead somewhere because they chose to stand up for their rights.

After several weeks of protests by Rev. King and Rev. Reese, as they led marchers from Brown Chapel AME Church to the courthouse in trying to gain the right to vote, many things happened. There were several weeks of Blacks being jailed, beaten, starved, and even killed in early 1965. Boynton said that it had been reported to the SCLC that more than 2,000 men, women, and children had been imprisoned in Selma and the adjacent counties of Perry, Marion, and Wilcox.

Mrs. Boynton continued to describe in disbelief what she had heard from the people around the city: Everyone came into her office explaining how their relatives, friends, and children were being treated in the county jails and prison camps. It was deplorable according to Mrs. Boynton.

Their meals at the camp consisted of cornbread with sand and rocks in it. The syrup and coffee had salt. Mrs. Boynton noted that there weren't any toilets and there was only one open stool for the people to use. And the women, Mrs. Boynton explained, had to form a wall around each other to keep from being exposed. Some black folks said that it reminded them of how they used to hear stories about slaves coming across the Atlantic ocean, packed like sardines on slave ships from Africa.

In another example, Amelia described what was essentially a holding cage where Selma citizens were dehumanized. Black folks had to lay down on the ground at the prison camp because there were no rooms or beds to be found. Many slept while standing, with chains wrapped around their arms and waists.

The guards also made the men stand in single file with each person's nose in the hair of the one in front of him. If anyone moved, the guard struck him in his privates with a cattle prod. She sighed as she thought about it. But that wasn't all, as Mrs. Boynton explained. The women had to sleep on a wet floor. Such evil treatment was similar to that ordered by Hitler and that experienced on slave ships from Africa, as their "cargo" arrived in a new country that was controlled by the "White Masa's" of the time.

Meanwhile by February 1, 1965, Dr. King was arrested in Selma and held in the county jail for leading the January 18 demonstration. In addition, Rev. Ralph Abernathy, SNCC workers Frank Soracco and William Hall were arrested for parading the street without a permit as they marched to the county courthouse. Dallas County, Alabama courthouse records show that 450 high school students were arrested that same day on the same charges as they marched to protest the difficulties their parents had in registering to vote.

The arrest of Dr. King stirred up a lot of people across the country. He'd become known across the country and around the world for his leadership role in the victories from the Montgomery Bus Boycott of the mid-1950s and the Civil Rights Act of 1964. The bombing and killing of four little black girls at a Birmingham church during a Sunday morning worship service would play a pivotal role in the passing of the civil rights bill.

People began to come to Selma to offer their services in whatever way was needed. Rev. Andrew Young was Dr. King's aide, and with his guidance, there was a large meeting held at Brown Chapel AME Church that was led by a group of people from Washington, D.C. This included congressmen who were in Selma to visit unofficially.

King gave instructions from his jail cell to keep the focus of national attention on Selma, according to Mrs. Boynton. King had Rev. Abernathy call Sammy Davis to do a Sunday benefit in Atlanta to raise money for the Alabama voting rights project. King often told key supporters of the movement where funding was needed most. He further explained to Abernathy that entertainers tended to respond with their time and money better when he was in jail or in a crisis.

"I was to drive to the Montgomery airport and lead the group of congressmen back to Selma. The congressman would ask at city hall to see Dr. King. I was to sign his bond, and the entire group would come to my house for a meeting," Amelia said. Upon King's arrival at the airport there awaited fifteen congressmen, eight other friends and a batch of news reporters with cameras, tape recorders and writing tablets in hand, ready to report to the world Selma's fight for voting rights.

The drive back to Selma went as planned. A few of the SNCC and SCLC organizational members met up with the distinguished group arriving from the airport at city hall. Attempts were made to enter the building from the side and front doors, but both were locked. Instead, everyone went in through the prison entrance as it was found to be open. It was a depressing, cold, and rainy kind of day. However, no one complained about the weather. In fact, the congressmen were quite optimistic.

Mayor Joe Smitherman met the group at the door with his hand on the doorknob, according to Mrs. Boynton. He did not want the congressmen to come into the building.

Smitherman was a tall, skinny, frightened, and uneasy type of man who had only been in office for a month, noted Amelia Boynton in *Bridge Across Jordan.* The young mayor made it clear that none of the 50-strong group were welcome in Selma. However, it was too late because by the time he finished rattling off a partisan speech, Congressman John Dow of New York was halfway inside the door. Other group members were still outside the building awaiting direction from Mrs. Boynton and Congressman Dow who had made it into Mayor Smitherman's office.

Amelia Boynton spoke up first, telling the mayor that the people couldn't hear what was being said so they would need to come in to listen. Mayor Smitherman agreed, allowing them to come in, but not the newsmen. Amelia agreed.

With the door now open, the congressmen commenced to file into the hall as if they were all getting ready to receive an official welcome to the speech from Smitherman. At least that was what the group members thought was about to happen. However, instead he went on a rampage to let them know that as the mayor of Selma that no racial problems or discrimination existed here. "Everyone gets along here, and outsiders are not welcome in this city!" Smitherman yelled.

At this point, Congressman William Fitts Ryan of New York and the others said that everyone had come to see Dr. King, Mrs. Boynton recollected. The mayor responded that no one would be allowed to see King unless he were out on bond. Another congressman replied that no one wanted to get him out of jail, they just wanted to see him. "Well, no one can just see him," was the major response, Mrs. Boynton recalls.

After all the congressmen had entered the hall, the mayor slowly eased into a larger hallway where he intentionally distanced himself from them. Then out of nowhere came a series of questions that the congressmen wanted Mayor Smitherman to answer. Why were Blacks barred from registering and voting? Another asked about the common pattern of discrimination, while yet another wanted to know about the inhuman treatment of the demonstrators. The mayor nervously answered the questions, but found himself in a difficult position with the lawmakers of the nation. "He embarrassed himself," Mrs. Boynton articulated.

By that time, the city and county attorneys had arrived and told the mayor that he didn't have to answer the group's question. However, the mayor refused to listen to the attorneys and continued trying to respond to the questions being asked. After about half an hour, Mayor Smitherman was continuing to argue with these officials about Selma and the condition they felt it was in.

Amelia stood by and watched Smitherman make a fool of himself. There was no way for him to clean up the lies he was telling the congressmen. Finally, out of nowhere one of the attorneys returned and took the mayor by the elbow as if he were a child in distress. Smitherman continued to snap back at the congressman, newsmen and others in the group as he walked away. All the dignitaries witnessed this scene unfold in amazement and disbelief, Amelia concluded.

In the meantime, while this was all happening, the SCLC made the bond payment for Dr. King's release. Shortly after that, Selma's safety director, Captain Wilson Baker, came and announced that Dr. King had been released. But the congressmen wondered where he was. Captain Wilson informed the group that King had slipped out the front door while Major Smitherman was addressing them.

"When the group reached my house on Lapsley Street, Dr. King was there awaiting us for the meeting,"[69] Mrs. Boynton said. There stood bravely some of the most intellect minds of the great country—with dignity and justice together in unity. Amongst the local black leaders and SCLC members were congressmen Jonathan B. Bingham, James H. Scheuer, Ogden Reid, William Fitts Ryan, Joseph Y Resnick and John Dow from New York. In addition, there were Jeffery Cohelan, Kenneth W. Dyal, August F. Hawkins, and Don Edwards from California, Weston E. Vivan and Charles Mathias from Maryland, and John Conyers, Jr. from Michigan. In their midst, also from New York, was Representative Clayton Powell. There were also many others, whose presence spoke volumes as

[69] Boynton Robinson, 251.

they, too, stood proud at the conference, representing those leaders who were unable to make it down to Selma.[70] Amelia couldn't believe what she was seeing with her own eyes. All of these dignitaries were present at her home at 1315 Lapsley Street.

Amelia's Lapsley Street home became immensely popular during the movement. She explained that before she and Bill had become the owners, it was owned by a former state demonstration agent by the name of Mrs. Rosa Jones Ballard. Ballard had worked very closely with Booker T. Washington, Tuskegee Institute's founder. She had also worked with Thomas Campbell, the first United States Department of Agriculture's Director for the seven lower states. Both Mr. Campbell and Mrs. Booker T. Washington were among the many visitors at the Boyntons' home in Selma.

Everyone's eyes in the neighborhood were focused on 1315 Lapsley Street. As they gathered around in the yard, the congressmen told them that a meeting to talk about voting rights in Selma was about to start. The meeting began right after Amelia and some of the ladies of SCLC finished serving dinner.

Dr. King, the SCLC representatives, and Mrs. Boynton were chosen to talk about what was happening in Selma so that the congressmen would have information to take back to Washington. After the congressmen had heard from the speakers, they disseminated and talked with the whites and blacks in attendance for further clarification. As Amelia Boynton noted in her many speeches and engagements around this country and the world, it

---

[70] Ibid., 251.

was because of this drafting of a right-to-vote bill at her kitchen table with Dr. King and others that later led to a ratification of the bill the following August.

However, at the present time, all was not well in Selma and surrounding counties for those who tried to register to vote. Blacks were being beaten, jailed, lynched and fired from their jobs. And, according to historical documents of the incident in Marion, Alabama, after a large gathering, Jim Lee Jackson had been shot and murdered by one of Governor Wallace's state troopers. Because of these atrocities Selma, began to gain even more publicity around the world.

Many people wanted to get involved and show their resentment toward the injustices committed against African Americans. On March 6, 1965, both whites and blacks from around Alabama came together to protest the ongoing wrong treatment of black people in Selma.

White citizens, including businessowners and professional men and women, ministers and laymen, came in groups to support the African Americans' plea for the right to vote, Mrs. Boynton proclaimed. The white churches feared for their congregation lives so they finally gathered in a black church (the Reformed Presbyterian) to rest before marching up to the county courthouse two-by-two, as Amelia details in *Bridge Across Jordan*. Later the Concerned White Citizens of Alabama (CWCA) met up at the courthouse where they were harassed by a gang of white rebels.

With all the demonstrations, conferences, pleading and confrontations, the registration board and white supremacists in Selma continued to block blacks from registering by beating them down both mentally and physically, Mrs. Boynton affirms.

It was long-established by the DCVL, Bill and Amelia Boynton, SCLC, SNCC and Dr. King and others that the core of the problem had started with elected officials at the state capital. And taking the grievances and placing them in the hands of Governor George Wallace in Montgomery was the only way to address concerns in the black communities. African Americans meant business about having the right to register and vote. The march would begin on Sunday March 7, 1965.

Dr. King and Mrs. Boynton and others were aware that the city knew of their plans to take to the streets and march up to the capitol building in Montgomery, Alabama. The catalyst for the march was the death of 26-year-old Jimmy Lee Jackson on February 26. Because of the news and media coverage of the unfolding incidents and ongoing events in Selma, people from all over the country began to trickle into the city to assist with the voting drive and voter registration.

Still, there would be no let up from the county board of registrars. Governor Wallace's spiral-bound notebook of legal questions for blacks to answer still stood in the way of them registering. At the same time, according to Dr. King, in Washington, Congress was still trying to get a voting rights bill passed.

There would be no alternative left now but to walk 50 miles to the capital not to ask or plead, but to demand the right to register and vote, Amelia concluded.

The night before the march, everyone gathered at Brown Chapel A.M.E. Church for a pep talk that was given to the citizens, asking them to march even if it meant giving up life. "I was afraid of being killed and I said to myself that I cannot pay the supreme price because I have given too much already,"[71] Mrs. Boynton emotionally recalled. She reflected on the past 30 or so years with all the fighting, lynching, killings and unsolved murders which had occurred in Selma—the many who had given the ultimate sacrifice—their lives. Amelia Boynton decided that she would continue and march even if the cost was her life. She thought and prayed quietly by herself at the church. Afterward, Mrs. Boynton felt a heavy burden had been lifted from her mind and she knew she was ready to suffer and die for the right to vote if need be.

The day had arrived and Amelia rose early to cook breakfast for the fifteen guests staying in her home. The strategy had been mapped out on which route to take from the church. Afterward, she arrived early at Brown Chapel to see if any assistance was needed before the march. "I knew I wasn't going to march all the way. I had planned on marching until they got to the first place where they were going to camp, and then I would have to go back home, "[72] Amelia explained. Her house had been turned over to Dr. King and his staff and half of Mrs. Boynton office had been given over to the SCLC so she knew that there was no way for her to make to make the five-day march. As everyone began the march, a line of adults and children wished them all Godspeed.

An untold number of law enforcement officers from the city, county and state stood by watching. No one knew what was going to happen,

---

[71] Ibid., 253.
[72] Notley.

upon approaching the Edmund Pettus Bridge, there they stood: Sheriff Clark, his deputies, and a posse. Then, from out of nowhere, white men dressed in denim corduroy farm clothes were ready for battle. "Keep the Niggers in their place!" they yelled, just as everyone began crossing the bridge. The marchers looked on in astonishment and continued crossing the bridge.

"I was walking next to my friend, Marie Foster, and she looked at me wondering what was going to happen next,"[73] Mrs. Boynton explained.

Each officer was equipped with cans of gas, guns, sticks and cattle prods. They knew that something was about to happen because beyond the officers were men on horses ready to beat up on some Niggers. Abruptly, all the marchers became aware of what was happening since up to then, most had only gotten a little ways across the bridge. Then the march came to a halt. A state trooper by the name of Cloud started to talk, saying, "Go back to your church!"

A man named Hosea Williams spoke up, "May I have something to say?"[74] Mrs. Boynton described.

"No!" the state Trooper screamed. "Not a word out of anyone. Charge on them, men!" And so they came from the right, left, front and sides, starting to beat everyone, Mrs. Boynton remembered frantically. Amelia explained that she was the type of person who didn't know how to run, couldn't run and didn't run. So, she just froze.

---

[73] Ibid.
[74] Notley.

She commented that it was not because of fear. Rather, it was due to her amazement at seeing all these people being beaten by local policemen, state troopers, Sheriff Clark, his deputies, and his auxiliary deputies known as "possemen." The thought running through Mrs. Boynton mind was that this supposed to be nothing but a peaceful march. It was for negro citizens to exercise their constitutional right to assemble peaceably and petition the government for full citizenship with voting rights.

Amelia describes what she saw first-hand as a citizen looking on as a marcher: "They were standing erect, they were dressed in their uniform, they had clubs, they had cattle prods—one in one hand, and one in the other. Then, they had on a gas mask, ready for whatever that was getting ready to happen. And there were some people on horses."

The troopers had on gas masks, and stood with gas guns in hand. They began to shoot gas at everyone and as people were beaten, blood began to spatter on their clothes and on the highway. Some tumbled from side to side as they were beaten to the ground with clubs, while others were beaten back across the bridge. "Is this humane?" Amelia pondered.

As the marchers fell, they would get back up and keep running back across the river with broken limbs. Finally, one of the state troopers noticed Amelia as she stood frozen as if in another dimension. He yelled, "Run!" But Amelia just gave him a dirty look because she wasn't about to run.

Amelia carefully described the beating that she took from the trooper. He viciously clubbed her repeatedly across her neck, back, and shoulders and then he shot tear gas directly into her face causing her to collapse and fall to the ground unconscious.

Amelia recalled others telling her that her attacker had called for another deputy whom he had the "damn leader." She was also told that the guy standing over her with a stick in some of the pictures that were taken was the one who did the beating.

Witnesses also explained to her that the officers had taken a canister of gas and pumped it all over her. Amelia believes that a cap given to her by her friend, Margaret Moore, is what saved her face and nose from severe injury—and in retrospect, her life. Amelia only heard these stories from other witnesses as she had remained unconscious.

They also told her that after they had dragged out the people who had broken limbs and so forth, that same trooper called out to Sheriff Jim Clark: "There's someone dead over here. Call and send for an ambulance." But the sheriff yelled out! "No! I'm not sending an ambulance anywhere! If anybody is dead over there, let buzzards eat 'em!"[75] Mrs. Boynton intensely explained.

Amelia was taken to the aid station at Brown Chapel—which had been swamped with the injured. However, after she didn't respond to attempts to wake her up, she was rushed to Good Samaritan Hospital.

According to print, news and radio reports that documented "Bloody Sunday," by the end of the day, 100 of the 600 marchers had required medical attention for fractured skulls, broken teeth and limbs, gas poisoning, and whiplash,

Mrs. Boynton finally woke up in the hospital after being unconscious

---

[75] Ibid., 9.

from the beating she took at the Edmund Pettus Bridge. She asked about what had happened. The marchers explained to her that a white minister had demanded for the sheriff to send for an ambulance to pick up all the wounded from the protest at the bridge. Then told her that a black man finally yelled at Sheriff Clark, telling him that there would be vengeance—with a plan to kill him and a riot to burn down the city. It was only then that ambulances were permitted in to pick up the injured.

Then Amelia went on to give more details about what she could remember happened on that day, now known historically as "Bloody Sunday." She didn't personally remember much after the blow to the head, but she did recall what they told her had happened.

All of a sudden it came to her mind what she recalled in the hospital. The voice she had heard screaming in her mind while in the hospital bed was that loud bullhorn the sheriff had used as he ordered marchers to turn around as gas was being sprayed out by men wearing gasmasks. Amelia recalled lying on a hospital bed in the emergency room looking around at all the wounded being bandaged up. As she remembered it, the scene in her mind was of a slaughterhouse of victims on Highway 80 across the Edmund Pettus Bridge.

"If I had any idea that the state troopers would use the kind of brutality they did, I would have felt compelled to give up my church duties altogether to lead the line. It was one of those developments that none of us anticipated. We felt that the state troopers, who had been severely criticized over their terrible acts two weeks earlier even by conservative Alabama papers, would never again engage in that kind of violence,"[76] Dr.

---

[76] Stanford: Chapter 26: Selma "The Martin Luther King, Jr Research and Education Institute"

King said in a speech at Stanford University.

Amelia couldn't figure out what happened to Dr. King. Why wasn't he at the march? But someone told her that a call had been made to Dr. King and he that he was supposed to have led the march. Dr. King later said in a speech at Stanford University that he never forgot the pain of guilt for not being there after he heard of the immoral acts done against nonviolent demonstrators that Sunday, March 7.

Dr. King had been juggling his schedule and responsibilities as the pastor of Ebenezer Church in Atlanta. He had already missed the prior two Sundays, so he had felt compelled to be there that Sunday morning, and again that night for the Lord's Supper and baptismal service at 7:30 p.m.. Originally, the plan was for Dr. King to take a charter plane from Atlanta to Montgomery and then lead the march from Selma to Montgomery. He would spend three or four hours leading the march and then take a charter plane back for the evening services.

"But when Governor Wallace issued his ban on the march, it was a speech from most of my associates that the state troopers would deal with the problem by arresting all of the people in the line. We never imagined that they would use the brutal methods to which they resorted to repress the march. I concluded that if I were arrested it would be impossible for me to get back to the evening service at Ebenezer to administer the Lord's Supper and baptism. Because of this situation, my staff urged me to stay in Atlanta and lead a march on Monday morning,"[77] recalled Dr. King. This

https://kinginstitute.stanford.edu/king-papers/documents/address-conclusion-selma-montg
[77] Stanford University, "The Martin Luther King Jr, Research and Education Institute," https://kinginstitute.stanford.edu/chapter-26-selma

decision resulted in him having an agonized conscience for not being there after he heard of the devious acts perpetrated against nonviolent demonstrators. Therefore, he knew that he had to lead the march on the following Tuesday.

Dr. King felt the march on Tuesday, March 9 illustrated the dilemma of the battles ahead. It would have been unthinkable not to at least try to march again. However, Dr. King knew that whether marching to Montgomery or to a more limited point within the city of Selma could not be determined in advance. The only certain thing was that it had to begin so that a confrontation with injustice would take place in full view of the millions looking on throughout the nation.

Many months after the march, Amelia continued to have throat problems:. They discovered that her esophagus was permanently scorched and scarred by the teargas. This changed her voice from a lyric-soprano to mezzo-soprano, she stated. Mrs. Boynton hadn't let things get her down at this point. In fact, her spirit was uplifted even more to realize what it meant to sing one of the old negro songs which made her feel like freedom was on the way.

CHAPTER 21
THE FOOT SOLDIERS, MARCHERS ARRIVE IN SELMA

Then, we had Governor George Wallace. George Wallace put up every hurdle he possibly could because he saw that we were fighting for civil rights, we were fighting for the right to vote. And he said, one time during a national televised speech, "Segregation today. Segregation tomorrow. Segregation forever."

—AMELIA BOYNTON

They came from all over the world in support of the march—students, clergy, and housewives, both White and Blacks, had all the beatings across the Edmund Pettus Bridge on television. Across the country, Freedom Movement activists responded and were ready to take a stand. Mobilization and support demonstrations at federal buildings across the state began to protest because of the blood baths of Blacks being beaten in Selma. CBS and NBC, along with newspapers across the country, provided gruesome coverage. The media continued to flood the airwaves with reports showing people of all races and nationalities traveling to Selma by trains, planes, busses, and cars.

Mrs. Boynton described the diverse group of races who came together for one purpose—to put an end to the struggle, suffering, and sacrifice that Blacks had endured in the South because of not having the right to vote.

In the meantime, Dr. King arrived back in Selma, calling for a meeting with SCLC and SNCC organizations to strategize a plan to move forward with the march. As King talked with the groups, he explained that he had met with the President of the United States, but he left disappointed because he was asked not to march to Montgomery, as Mrs. Boynton recollects. But the people were in Selma from all over the United States and even from abroad to help in whatever way they could. So Dr. King couldn't simply back out of the march, even if he had wished to, Boynton noted.

The news media would prove most engaged when trying to get the films out of the Selma "blood bath" that had taken place right before their very eyes. Mrs. Boynton believes it was the quick response and reporting about Selma that mobilized the country to take notice and protest to their congressmen, city and state officials that something had to be done about this struggle for freedom. On top of that, Sunday night programs around the country were interrupted with special news bulletins showing footage of the atrocities in Selma.

Amelia, along with others, suggested to King that the march should continue even if it didn't end up advancing that far. By mid-afternoon, more than 3000 marchers had assembled at the playground next to Brown Chapel Church, waiting for directions from Dr King. "I have been agonizing and I've made my choice. I have decided that it is better to die on the highway than to make a butchery of my conscience,"[78] King said.

Although Amelia was still feeling the effects of the gas and the blows to her head from "Bloody Sunday," she was not content with staying in the hospital for further evaluation. Instead, she made her decision to leave the hospital and return to the church at 3 p.m. on March 9.

Dr. King decided that there would be a march later that day. This time, on that perfect, warm and sunny day, King told the crowd, it would be all the way to Montgomery. The crowd responded with applause and cheers; What he hadn't told the marchers was that he had agreed to turn the march around when ordered to halt.

Surrounding Dr. Martin Luther King Jr were many prominent people from all over the country. Mrs. Boynton noted that the marchers included clergy, actors, scientists, and celebrities from many different professions. The marchers strolled down the street, past the George Washington Carver Homes—a Black housing project that gave a panorama of the African Americans' low income homes that led into Selma's business district.

People, both Black and White, lined the sidewalks as the marchers passed. Some of the Whites were muttering obnoxious words and chanting for the Nigger supporters to go back home. The marchers paid no attention and kept on walking.

A local deputy officer frowned and stopped traffic to allow everyone onto Broad Street toward the bridge. Once across the bridge, the marchers stopped where they had been attacked the previous Sunday and said a

---

[78] Boynton Robinson, 258.

prayer that was led by Rev. Abernathy, Bishop Lord, Dr. Docherty, and Rabbi Hirsch. At the foot of the bridge, a federal marshal halted their progress and read aloud "King" Judge Johnson's injunction. Dr. King noted that he was aware of the injunction, but then resumed the march.

When the marchers reached the crest of the bridge, more than 500 state Alabama troopers were lined up behind barricades across the 80 West highway. State Trooper Major John Cloud ordered the protesters to stop. King made the case for their march but Cloud refused to listen to his reasons.

Amelia vividly described how that suddenly Major Cloud shouted, "Troops withdraw!"[79] They pulled back and opened the road to Montgomery.

Everyone around King awaited his command. However, sensing a trap to lure him into violating the injunction and providing justification for the police to attack, Amelia remembered that Dr. King shouted, "Let's go back to the church now!" With no dispute from the marchers, they made a U-turn all returned to Brown Chapel.

For the most part, Amelia recalled that the marchers felt sort of a relief that the police did not attack them. However, others felt betrayed, disgusted and angry because they were pumped up and ready to fight to the death if the troops would have attacked them.

Back at Brown Chapel Church, people were still arriving from the

---

[79] "Civil Rights Movement History & Timeline,"(Selma & the March to Montgomery) pg. 37/67 https://www.crmvet.org/tim/timhis65.htm#1965

North, East and West and Dr. King asked the Northerner supporters who could stay in Selma to do so. He told everyone at the gathering that soon there would be another march. Everyone seemed to be stirred by the charismatic preacher's comments, Mrs. Boynton reminisces in her memoir *Bridge Across Jordan*.

As night fell, among those who came to Selma and remained after the march would be the white Unitarian ministers James Reeb and Orloff Miller of Boston and Clark Olsen of Berkeley. Since there was much confusion among the Northerners who came to Selma to help with the march, some didn't get the memo concerning the do's and don'ts in Selma after dark came. Local Blacks would inform all newcomers to the city concerning places they could go into and other places where Negroes weren't welcome including business establishments, restaurants, and churches.

Reverends Reeb, Olsen, and Miller went into a black area to have supper in a white café on Washington street. When they saw the looks of some of the Whites, they decided to go back to Walker's, a black café. After eating there, they started to walk back toward the Movement offices at Alabama and Franklin streets, and passed by the Silver Moon Café, which was a hangout for Klansmen and possemen. As they did, four white men with baseball bats and rough-and-ready homemade clubs stepped from the shadows and attacked the three ministers.

"Hey, you Niggers!" they hollered as they struck both Olsen and Miller, and bludgeoned Reeb in the head. Reeb and Miller dropped to the ground as they continued to be brutally beaten: As their attackers ran away, they shouted, "Now you know what it's like to be a real Nigger!"[80]

Miller and Olsen were bleeding, but weren't as seriously injured as Reeb who was dazed, confused, and could barely see. They made their way back to the SCLC office, about two blocks away.

As Amelia Boynton points out, this was her office and many workers were still there when the ministers arrived. She and Diane Nash went next door and asked the director of the funeral home to get an ambulance. Dr. William H. Dinkins, a black doctor, came and assisted Mr. Reeb to Burwell, the only African American-owned-and-operated hospital in the area.

The black doctor at Burwell determined the Reeb needed immediate neurosurgery. Unfortunately, the nearest emergency unit willing to do an operation of that kind was 90 miles away in Birmingham. However, that facility refused to treat him without an advance cash payment of $150, according to the "Civil Rights Movement History and Timeline" report.

Somehow, Mrs. Boynton and Ms. Nash managed to come up with the money and the hearse rushed Reeb, Olsen, and Miller north to Birmingham. Upon arrival at University Hospital, Reeb was diagnosed with a massive skull fracture, a blood clot, and a pneumonia infection. The doctors knew that they could not save him. Tragically, breaking news around the world reported that Reeb had died while rallying at a civil rights meeting being held at Brown Chapel on March 14. Various Bloody Sunday videos detailed this horrific murder, as marchers spoke of the night Reeb was beaten to death while walking in the downtown streets of Selma.

---

[80] Ibid., 39.

Reeb's memorial service was delivered by Dr. King at Brown Chapel as the march to protest his murder continued to be block by a court injunction. This injunction stopped marchers from going to the Dallas County courthouse to complain about Reeb's death and the right to register to vote.

Meanwhile, all over the country, people were protesting about the treatment of human beings in Selma on March 7, including city, state and federal government officials. Along with others, Amelia said she suggested that the march should continue even though Dr. King was still disturbed and in a dilemma because of what the President of the United States had asked of him—not to march or attempt to go the 50 miles to Montgomery.

In many documented videos, Amelia explained that people had come from all over the United States and from abroad because they wanted to help however they could. She continued to let everyone know that Dr. King did not want to disobey federal regulations or the request from President Johnson. Nor did he want to disappoint the thousands of people who had come to Selma to participate in the march. It was settled, she said. Everyone would assemble at Brown Chapel Church and await instructions from King.

As the country watched it played out on national television, President Johnson took the rally cry of African American, "we shall overcome," into the halls of Congress. Johnson reminded them of what he called "a crippling legacy of bigotry and injustice." As a result, Americans in this country and abroad would see immediate legislation enacted to remove every barrier of injustice against citizens trying to register to vote.

Meanwhile, Reeb's assailants were identified as Namon O'Neal Heggie, his brother William, Elmer L. Cook, and R. B. Kelley whose ages ranged from 30 to 32 according to local city, state, and local reports covering the minister's murder. Court documents confirmed their arrest for assault and battery and they were all be arraigned for murder and released on $5,000 bond. They were tried under an 1870 conspiracy law that would have given them a maximum penalty of ten years in prison and a $5,000 fine. "I sat in the Selma courthouse and was disgusted, though not surprised, to see that there were no black people on the jury: jurors consisted of friends of the murders, and I was told that one was an in-law of one of them,"[81] Amelia Boynton recalled.

During the jury trial for Reeb, Amelia noticed that the defendants were nonchalant. And just as Amelia had expected, the jury's verdict was "not guilty" thus the state freed them. The men, their family members and friends cheered, gave high fives, and shook hands with each other. This was justice at its finest in Selma. But unfortunately, she was not just speaking sarcastically. Rather, it's a statement that could be justified even today in the twenty-first century as an argument could be made that not much has changed in Selma since that time. But, of course, there is the right to full citizenship now as well as the right to register and vote.

[81] Boynton Robinson, 262.

CHAPTER 22
MARCH 20, 1965 PILGRIMAGE, SELMA TO MONTGOMERY

On March 20, I spent a couple hours at Brown Chapel Church, where instructions were being given to marchers, then went to my office, where SCLC officials were busy getting out last-minute notices for the greatest march on earth.

—AMELIA BOYNTON ROBINSON

The stage was set. Carloads of state troopers and a swarm of possemen (aka a white hate group) were in Selma like an army. Local students, SNCC activists, bishops, ministers, rabbis, wives of U. S. Senators, union leaders, and students from famous universities had arrived at Brown Chapel A.M.E. Church. Known today as the Mecca for the voting rights movement, there was a lot of socializing going on between local Blacks northern Whites, and Hispanics as everyone waited for the green light from President Johnson to begin the 50-mile march to Montgomery that had been attempted on both March 7 and 8. In one of Amelia's interviews about the march, she explained that the aim was to lay a petition for African

Americans' right before Governor Wallace. Amelia, along with members of SNCC and SCLC patiently waited to hear what President Johnson's decision would be about the march. Up until then, Johnson had made every effort to persuade King not to march because he was primarily focused on the Vietnam War at the time. Everyone had left Mrs. Boynton's office in downtown Selma after waiting for hours to hear what President Johnson's decision would be regarding the march to the state capitol in Montgomery.[82]

Amelia would awake the next morning to her home filled with SCLC and SNCC group members who had spent the night strategizing the water drop-off and food points, the security look-out duty, and alternate avenues of approach to Montgomery in case there are attacks from blood-thirsty race groups. She prepared breakfast for the freedom fighters and left a key so that they could have access to move about in and out of the house as needed.

Amelia left her home on Lapsley street and arrived back at their real estate and employment agency where more leaders of SCLC and SNCC were waiting on Dr. King's arrival and President Johnson's decision concerning the march to the capitol in Montgomery. All of a sudden a SCLC group member rushed into the office with the news that President Johnson had given the greenlight to march.

President Johnson ordered Governor Wallace and the state of Alabama to carry out and protect the march. Furthermore, the President ordered the

---

[82] "Civil Rights Movement History & Timeline," Selma & the March to(1965)Montgomery https://www.crmvet.org/tim/timhis65.htm#1965

federal government to provide whatever assistance the state required.

Minutes later, Mrs. Boynton arrived at her office where she received a second summons by the same deputy sheriff who had given her the first one with a smirk on his face. This summons was designed to block the DCVL and the SCLC from carrying black people back and forth on minibuses after their demonstrations back to their residences in Selma and the surrounding rural counties. Although Amelia didn't realize it at first, she finally put it all together. Blacks not riding Selma city buses was beginning to cause a slight economic pinch that was being felt in the city's coffers. Little did they know, Amelia pointed out, most Blacks had stopped riding the city buses long before the end of December in 1964—which was when DCVL and SCLC started running a minibus line themselves.

Without warning, Mrs. Boynton received yet a third complaint within the same hour when the sheriff came back to their and threw another summons on her desk, this time with despair written all over his face. This time, Mrs. Boynton noted, it was an injunction to stop the marchers from camping in Lowndes County on a Minter plantation that was being leased by a black farmer from a white owner.

Meanwhile, Dr. King received the news that President Johnson had given the greenlight to move forward with the march. King was very excited and ordered the SNCC to give him a report on the logistics and rest areas along the way. He mingled with his friends, dignitaries, and foot soldiers from near and far who had arrived to be a part of the pilgrimage from Selma to Montgomery.

As the sun beamed brightly, with a cool breeze to bring comfort,

Amelia estimated that a crowd of more than 3,000 marchers lining up to walk two-by-two through GWC project complex, and on to Sylvan Street—known today as Martin Luther King Street. They were well-informed and intuitive concerning what was about to go down.

The march started at 1 o'clock sharp as they headed off toward the Edmund Pettus Bridge, which had been named for a Confederate general and Grand Dragon of the KKK. Leading the march, Amelia could see the American flags and a United Nations flag flying high.

As reported on local television and radio stations across the country, Dr. King, Rabbi Abraham Heschel, UN leader Ralph Bunche, Episcopal Bishop Richard Millard, and other luminaries put on some colorful flower leis that had been distributed by the Hawaiian contingent. Among the front ranks, Amelia recognized Cager Lee (grandfather of Jimmie Lee Jackson), DCVL President F. D. Reese, Dr. King, and SNCC Chairman John Lewis. But the bulk of the marchers were mostly Blacks from Selma and Alabama's Black Belt counties. Amelia could be seen on the third row from the right, dressed in her Sunday-best with an off-white scarf and hat on her head.

As they approach the crest of the bridge, Mrs. Boynton, her dear friend Marie Foster, and their fellow foot soldiers saw just what President Johnson had promised—the United States Army waiting to escort the marchers all the way to Montgomery. She could see two helicopters overhead, ready to engage and chaperone from the heavens. Dr. King, Amelia and the marchers walked past crowds of white hecklers who jeered, cursed, and waving Confederate battle flags. The army soldiers, with bayonets fixed, were holding down their rage, feeling hopeless because none of them were able to penetrate the crowd in order to whip, beat and maybe kill them some "Niggers" or some white "Nigger-lovers" who were protesting too.

Video footage and historical photos have shown white hate groups riding along the march route in cars with "I hate niggers" and "Yankee trash go home" painted on the side. Some Northerners were shocked by the verbal violence as screams poured from the hate groups. Local newspapers raised eyebrows by claiming that the nuns and white women were only there for sexual orgies with black men. However, Movement activists who had experienced this form of "southern decorum" in state after state for years were not surprised.

The initial leg of the 54-mile march was short—only seven miles to the first campsite. Thousands of marchers would need to be taken back to Selma, leaving only those permitted on the next two phases through Lowndes County. By 7 a.m., the 300 officially permitted marchers allowed for safety reasons by President Johnson were on the road for the 16-mile race to the second campsite. Other marches would join them later where highway 80 split into four lanes upon entering Montgomery County.

Little did the marchers know that the 300-person limit was for their own protection. This number, being relatively small, would give the U. S. military and air policing more control and make it easier to spot possible snipers and bomb traps designed to kill marchers. Foot soldiers remained vigilante in watching their surroundings because news reports were constantly coming out concerning the threat sniper attacks and bombs along the route. Since several bombs had already been disarmed in Birmingham, army demolition experts carefully inspected each bridge before the marchers arrived.

Marie Foster told Amelia that she'd made a vow to walk every step of the way. And she did just that. She and others would get stiff because of the rigorous long hours on their feet. In order to keep their minds off being killed by snipers, the rain, and cold muddy trails, marchers would sing civil rights hymns.

Amelia noticed that the teenagers were a great inspiration on the march as well. They kept everyone in high spirits with their silliness and their singing. Those songs could embody sadness, happiness, joy, or determination among many other feelings. The song "We Shall Overcome" quickly became the face of the movement. And, as a symbol of determination and freedom, some walked barefoot all the way to Montgomery.

Upon reaching the halfway point in Lowndes County, Amelia remembered that a minister had once told her that this county was worse than hell. That seemed to be a fact as illustrated by one of Amelia's stories. She recalled that in 1958, after testifying before the Civil Rights Commission in Montgomery, a local "Uncle Tom" had warned her not to come back because if she did it would be her death sentence. He told her that it would be a pleasure for him to kill her.

At the time, Lowndes County's population was 80% African American. However, as of 1965 not one African American was a registered voter. Amelia stated that according to Andy Young (Andrew Jackson Young Jr.), most Blacks in the county were either schoolteachers or sharecroppers—meaning that one way or another, whites had strings on them all. (Young was Dr. King's executive assistant at the time.)

The marchers could see that Lowndes County was mostly pastures, cotton, or corn fields, and was also filled with swampland having ghostly trees trailing long veils of Spanish moss, and dark slimy water with algae.

Some locals in the march began to talk about the story of "Bloody Lowndes," which was a tale of racially motivated land seizures, murders, eviction, exploitation, beating, arson, and frame up on false charges mainly by the county's white citizens. Like in other Black Belt counties, its Blacks were fed up with white supremacy hate crimes, but were afraid to fight back for fear of being killed.[83]

Amelia and the marchers crossed the Montgomery County line where the highway again widened to four lanes. Marchers who were sent back to Selma during the first leg of the journey could be seen on buses, cars, and pickup trucks headed to the rendezvous point—St. Jude Catholic Institute. Some would drop off to join the line of marchers that had grown from 300 to 500 and from 500 to nearly 1000.

The lines continued to grow the closer the marchers got to the outskirts of Montgomery. And it was 5000-strong by the time they reached St. Jude, where thousands more waited to greet them.

Amelia could see that people from all over the world had made it to St. Jude. They came by plane, bus, train, cars and some even by foot, she explained. Ultimately, there would be approximately 10,000 movement supporters.

---

[83] "Civil Rights Movement History & Timeline,"(Selma & the March to Montgomery) pg. 57/67. https://www.crmvet.org/tim/timhis65.htm#196 5

Everyone was excited to be there and they anticipated the entertainment that would take place that night. Celebrities of the stage and screen flew in by day to perform a free concert that evening called "Stars for Freedom." It was an improvised, outdoor stage assembled with coffins loaned by black funeral homes in the area that formed the floor. Luminaries included Mahalia Jackson, Dick Gregory, Joan Baez, Leonard Bernstein, Nina Simone, Nipsey Russel, Peter, Paul and Mary, Pete Seeger, Sammy Davis Jr., Odetta Davis, Ruby Dee, Ella Fitzgerald, and scores of others.

The next morning, March 25, light rain drifted down as thousands of marchers prepared for the final lap through Montgomery to the state capitol building. Amelia saw Dr. King making his way to the head of the march at St. Jude. The march had grown to around 12,000 who were singing freedom songs. By the time they reached Dexter Avenue, it was estimated that there were as many as 25,000 freedom marchers.

As they moved toward the capitol, most of the stores were deserted including the state building, where more than 10,000 employees worked—mainly Whites. (In contrast, most Blacks held menial jobs.)

Finally, Amelia and the marchers arrived at the platform on Dexter Avenue Baptist Church. In many of her live interviews, Amelia revealed how Andy Young had asked her to sit on the platform with King, himself among others. Amelia was pleased to be a distinguished guest on stage with some of the greatest thinkers and leaders in the world. "I saw at least 50,000 people marching down the street," Mrs. Boynton described.[84]

---

[84] Boynton Robinson, 270.

Andy Andrews then handed Amelia the petition to be read to the standing crowd of freedom marchers—the petition that they wanted to give to the governor face to face. Martin Luther King Jr., Roy Wilkins, Ralph Bunche, and other powerful figures all gave moving speeches to the cheers of the foot soldiers.

Dr. King delivered the main address—which is now known as the "Our God is Marching on Speech." He outlined the long history of racism and discrimination that blacks in Alabama, the South and in all of America were up against. King then honored the people of Selma who had fought, struggled, and sometimes died for freedom.

After King's speech, America spoke. The answer she gave was to let freedom ring for all people. Amelia looked back and pondered all that happened as part of the struggle for freedom. She reflected on her husband Samuel W. Boynton, C.J. Adams and Fannie Lue Haimer, and Martin Luther King Jr., who all died because of prior beatings or harassment, including assassination in the case of Dr. King.

The march from Selma to Montgomery put a small town on the map for its part in establishing equal voting rights for Blacks. However, this came at the cost of people being jailed, beaten, cattle-prodded, and gassed. Some lost their job, their homes, and even their lives in the city of Selma and Dallas County, both Blacks and Whites—All in the name of freedom.

CHAPTER 23
AFTER SELMA, THE NEXT CHAPTER

I lived to look back and evaluate the accomplishment from the struggle and set a timetable for the distance we have to go. Selma, Alabama, can be the candle of hope that will shine all over the world: as the light of justice, compassion, and love is exchanged for cattle prods, tear gas, billy clubs, and attack dogs.

—AMELIA BOYNTON ROBINSON

IT was 1965, and Selma was on the map as the city that fought for the full citizenship and equal voting rights not only for Blacks, but for all races. This changed the face of America moving forward into the twenty-first century with civil rights for all, no matter their racial heritage.

And it would be a pivotal time for Amelia as well.

She had already achieved a lot through being a key person working with Martin Luther King, Diane Nash, James Bevel, John Lewis, Andrew Young, Jesse Jackson and others of the Southern Christian Leadership Conference. She participated when plans were made to demonstrate for civil and voting rights. Mrs. Boynton's house on Lapsley street was where plans were mapped out with King and others. It was also where other SCLC members would meet to strategize the logistics for the march from Selma to Montgomery.

Moving forward to the year is 1969, it had been six years since Amelia's 27-year marriage to Bill had ended with his death. Amelia met Bob Billups during the holiday season in December of 1969 and married him one day after Christmas in 1970.

Bob was a musician and songwriter who had played with the big bands during the Great Depression. Those bands had included Duke Ellington and Earl "Fatha" Hines. After only about five years of marriage, Amelia lost Bob unexpectedly due to a boating accident in 1975.

Amelia Boynton eventually married a third time to former Tuskegee classmate James Robinson in 1976. She moved with him to Tuskegee after the wedding where James Robinson had accomplished many things in life after graduating from Tuskegee Institute with a degree in Agriculture.

During his time at that school, he had direct contact with Dr. George Washington Carver. But before moving on with his life after graduation, James lived in Tuskegee and maintained a small farm from which he furnished milk daily to Dr. Carver for over a year. Throughout his career, James had worked in various fields including as a physical therapist, in the U. S. Veterans Administration, and he also owned an interior decorating business in which he employed several others. James Robinson passed away in 1988 after complications from diabetes.

Taking on the name "Amelia Boynton Robinson," she continued her work in civil and human rights for all people. After the King years and the end of an era of hate and bigotry across the country, Boynton Robinson sought other avenues through which she could put her time and energy to work in helping to bring about a better world.

Since the civil right movement was not as active after the Martin Luther King Jr. death, Amelia Boynton Robinson in searching for other ways to be of service saw that much work was still needed in Selma and Tuskegee. One of the areas in which she got involved was to propose senior citizens' homes in Dallas County. This was a black housing project that had been approved by the representative for the Farmers Home Administration in Washington D. C. However, the final approval was held up by the Montgomery, Alabama FMHA official who had no intention of approving it in the first place.

Whether on the national, state, or city government levels, Amelia Boynton Robinson always expressed what she thought should be done for the poor and homeless—no matter their race.

She and her first husband, Bill, had been named "Mr. and Mrs. Civil Rights in Alabama." Some blacks, even including some friends, laughed and made fun of them in Selma. Others thought the Boyntons were crazy rabble-rousers for bothering with things over which they had no control and consequently they made it harder for black folks to survive.

The Boyntons had very few friends who truly trusted them even though they had fought for their rights for thirty plus years. It didn't matter to the Boyntons what the locals thought or felt because they knew that these folks were enslaved, bound, sharecroppers who needed help. Amelia and Sam were willing to do whatever it took help them through as they were in it for the long haul.

Amelia Boynton Robinson remembered what Samuel William "Bill " Boynton had spoken to her while on his deathbed. His condition resulted from a series of strokes and a heart attack. These were ultimately the cost he paid for the great danger, stress, and harassment of laying the groundwork for the civil rights movement that he and Amelia had spearheaded as early as the 1930s.

Amelia didn't let down the people of Selma. She was determined to keep fighting until they heard and understood. And Amelia refused to let down Bill. His death gave her the strength and the courage to go on and continue fighting for voting rights for local citizens and truly the world.

Together, the Boyntons spent decades laying the foundation for the movement that was led by Dr. Martin Luther King Jr.. They supported him when practically everyone else in Selma drew back in fear—including the local black church ministers. Robinson once said in an interview, "I have had worse things than that done to me when I was fighting for people's right to vote. Yes! I have been called a rabble-rouser, agitator. But because of my fighting. I was able to hand to the entire country the right for people to vote."[85]

In the mid 80's, when Amelia was way past retirement age and she could just go home and call it quits—she didn't. She still had work to do. God was not done with her yet. At 80-something she continued to write poems, plays and skits in Tuskegee for youth programs which enabled her to keep balance both physically and mentally.

---

[85] Amelia Boynton Robinson," Wikipedia.
https://en.wikipedia.org/wiki/Amelia_Boynton_Robinson

CHAPTER 24
MATRIARCH, VOTING RIGHTS, SCHILLER INSTITUTE

I live today in the city of Tuskegee where I went to college. Tuskegee University, founded by Dr. Booker T. Washington, is a key institution in the history of African Americans, as well as in my personal life.

—AMELIA BOYNTON ROBINSON

Amelia looked for other ways and places where her service might be needed. The march from Selma to Montgomery and the passage of the Civil Rights Act and voting rights for all had ended. But even at 80 years of age, Amelia still wanted more out of life. She wanted to continue the movement in other ways and to fight for life, liberty, and the pursuit of happiness.

Like the crusade that Martin Luther King Jr. had led, Amelia Boynton Robinson sought out another organization whose beliefs were focused specifically on humanity. She found herself getting involved with an several peace groups such as the Women's Strike for Peace, Women's International League for Peace and Freedom, the National Negro Women's Clubs, and other prominent organization. She even became an honorary member of the Delta Sigma Theta Sorority, Incorporated. While serving in those organizations, she still desired to reach out to others even more because of her love for her people and humanity, in general.

Appearing at a meeting in 1983 in Washington D. C., Robinson met Lyndon LaRouche—who was considered by some to be a highly controversial political figure in the Democratic Party. A year later, Amelia was asked to accept the nomination to serve as a founding board member of the LaRouche-affiliated Schiller Institute. She wondered if this organization might be the answer she was looking for.

In 1984, Amelia attended another meeting Lyndon LaRouche was the keynote speaker. Apprehensive, and yet a good listener, again LaRouche caught Amelia's attention with his discussion of the impact that the closing of factories, capping oil wells, and foreclosing on farmers would have on America and the world. Amelia saw with her own eyes that everything he said turned out to be true.

In the fall of the year, Amelia accepted the invitation to be on the advisory board of the Schiller Institute. The Schiller Institute, by definition, is an international organization that began in 1984. Helga Zepp-LaRouche was the board chairman of the Schiller Institute here in the United States and in Germany.

Being part of this organization, Amelia learned to become more open-minded about the edifice and function of government, including the wheeling and dealing, as well as the necessity of networking with people. She became more objective in her opinions about the government and the

Constitution and its history. She used constructive cognitive thinking before speaking about biased judges and ignorant juries that seemed to defy all reason and justice in their failure to make fair trial decisions based on the evidence presented.

As co-vice president/chairman of the Schiller Institute board, Amelia traveled on a fact-finding mission to West Berlin with several colleagues on behalf of the organization. These colleagues included LaRouche's Midwest Coordinator, Sheila Jones, and the former Borough President of Manhattan and a Schiller Institute board member, Hulan Jack.[86]

This was one year after Lyndon LaRouche had warned the Soviet Union that if they did not accept his Strategic Defense Initiative proposal as published by President Reagan in 1983, the Soviet system would collapse. Amelia and her delegation called for the reunification of the two Germanys and the demolition of the Berlin Wall. As forecast by LaRouche, the Berlin Wall fell five years later.

Then, a year later in the spring of 1990, Amelia returned to a reunited Germany where she would meet with thousands of citizens from both the former East and West. She began touring just the week before East Germany voted in a new non-communist government and was there to celebrate the reunification.[87]

In 1992, Amelia continued her travels by going to the embattled country of Croatia. There she met with members of the Croatian Mothers

---

[86] "The Schiller Institute/ICLC Conference." The Schiller Institute, September 1, 2001.https://archive.schillerinstitute.com/conficlc/2001/Labor%20Day/conf_sep_2001_mw_.html# mw%20speech.
[87] Ibid., 6.

for Peace and extended the Schiller Institute's support for their fight for justice and sovereignty, according to a recording documented by the Schiller Institute.

Over the next 10 years, Amelia participated in hundreds of Schiller Institute events around the world, inspiring those whom she met with her presence. Through this she was able to influence many school-age children. She lectured to thousands of children whom she inspired with her life's work, teaching the truth about America's history and impacting them with what they could do to make the world a better place.

From September to mid-November 2007, Amelia Boynton Robinson traveled to Sweden, Denmark, Germany, and Italy where she gave lectures to encourage others to join in on LaRouche's fight for a New Bretton Woods system and Eurasian Land-Bridge. This was the first system to control the value of money between different countries. It meant that each country had to have a monetary policy that kept the exchange rate of its currency within a fixed value, plus or minus one percent in terms of gold. The Eurasian Land-Bridge was sometimes called the New Silk Road, or Belt and Road Initiative which is the rail transport route to moving freight and passengers overland between Pacific seaports in the Russian Far East and China and seaports in Europe.

In her 90s, Amelia Boynton Robinson remained a vibrant leader, touring the nation and the world speaking for Schiller Institute on behalf of the principles of civil rights and human rights that she for which she had advocated for over nine decades.

Mrs. Robinson had incurred criticism for her association with Lyndon

H. LaRouche Jr., because of his former Marxist activities. Then after coming under scrutiny he was increasingly considered to be a part of the right-wing fringe. After a rigorous trial in federal courts, LaRouche served time in prison after being convicted in 1988 on charges including mail fraud and conspiring to defraud the Internal Revenue Service. When asked about problems of which she was aware within the Schiller Institute that she represented, Mrs. Robinson said her concerns were to advocate, speak, and teach about rights for the equal treatment and humanity for all mankind.

The Schiller Institute had been formed by Helga Zepp-LaRouche and Amelia Boynton Robinson, together with former Manhattan Borough President Hulan E. Jack. The organization reflected Dr. King's belief in the humane treatment of all mankind. Although some of the LaRouches' political views were controversial, to this day the Schiller Institute continues to advocate for economic development, culture, the issue of global warming, and moral questions facing civilization and humanity related to the continuation of the civil rights movement. Robinson retired as Chairman of the Board of the Schiller Institute in 2009 at the documented age of 104.

In 2014, the Selma City Council renamed five blocks of Lapsley Street "Amelia Boynton Robinson and Sam Boynton [Boyntons' Street]." Robinson was played by Lorraine Toussaint in the 2014 film *Selma*, which was about the Selma Voting Rights Movement and the Selma-to-Montgomery marches.[88]

---

[88] Biography. https://www.biography.com/people/amelia-boynton-21386459#civil-rights-

Mrs. Robinson continued her travels and speaking engagements up until her health would no longer permit it. "Amelia Boynton challenged an unfair and unjust system that kept African Americans from exercising their constitutionally protected right to vote," said Sewell, a Selma native who represented Alabama 7th Congressional District. Sewell continued, "She paved the way for me to accomplish all that I have today, and her legacy should inspire us not to take any of our rights for granted."[89]

Mrs. Robinson was invited by incoming President Barack Obama and Congresswoman Terri Sewell to hear him give the January 2015 State of the Union address. Although in a wheelchair, Amelia Boynton Robinson, joined President Obama as he, Congressman John Lewis, and others walked in procession across the Edmund Pettus Bridge on March 7, 2015. This marked the 50th anniversary of Bloody Sunday and the Selma Voting Rights Movement. It was the fulfillment of a lifetime dream for Amelia to see the first Black elected as the President of the U.S.

Amelia Boynton Robinson died on August 26, 2015 at the age of 110 according to newly found documents giving her correct age, according to Senator Hank Sanders. Her son Bruce Carver Boynton said of his mother's commitment to civil rights, "The truth of it is that was her life. That's what she was completely taken with." He added, that "she was a loving person, very supportive—but civil rights was her life."

Mrs. Boynton Robinson's words were heard loud and clear during the

---

movement. "Amelia Boynton"

[89] The Selma Times Journal. "Voting Rights leader attends State of Union." https://www.selmatimesjournal.com/2015/01/20/boynton-attends-state-of-union/

memorial service which was held in Selma. In a video that was played at the service, the attendees heard an audio clip that she had recorded during the last year of her life: "I wished to be cremated and would like my ashes to be interspersed in the waters of the Alabama River, directly along the Edmund Pettus Bridge."[90] Upon reaching the bridge, Bruce Boynton carried out his mother's wish, scattering her ashes.

The second final wish of Amelia Boynton Robinson was to rename the Edmund Pettus Bridge. Today, most African Americans feel that it should be named after a civil rights leader while others feel changing the name would be taking away from its historic significance. History points to the Confederate brigadier general and U. S. senator who was notorious for being one of the most vicious and murderous "Grand Dragons" of the Ku Klux Klan of his day. Nevertheless, in recent years, several petitions have been submitted to the federal government to change the name of the bridge from to something other than Edmond Pettus.

---

[90] Civil Rights Agenda. "Civil Rights Agenda."
https://civilrightsagenda.wordpress.com/tag/amelia-boynton-robinson-funeral/ page 5.

CHAPTER 25
HISTORY IN PICTURES

The Boynton Family in 1942: S.W. Boynton, Amelia Platts Boynton sons Bruce and Bill, Jr.

Amelia Boynton Robinson *(Photo provided by Boynton Family)*

(L) Amelia Boynton Robinson with President Lyndon B. Johnson at the signing of the Voting Rights Act, (R) with President Bill Clinton

Amelia Boynton Robinson with Dr. King's widow, Coretta Scott King, Mrs. King was featured speaker at a 1984 fundraising program at Tuskegee University. Also pictured are the president of the student council (far left) Tuskegee Major Johnny Ford.

Betty Strong Boynton: CEO, Founder, and Fundraiser for Amelia Boynton Robinson Foundation.

Bruce Boynton, Vice President co-founder Amelia Boynton Robinson Foundation

Photo provided by the Boynton family

Minister Louis Farrakhan visits Queen Mother. Amelia Boynton Robinson's home as Leon E. "Chief" Frazier and Dr. Ronald Scott McDoweell looks on *(Photo provided By Leon E. Frazier)*

(Google Image)

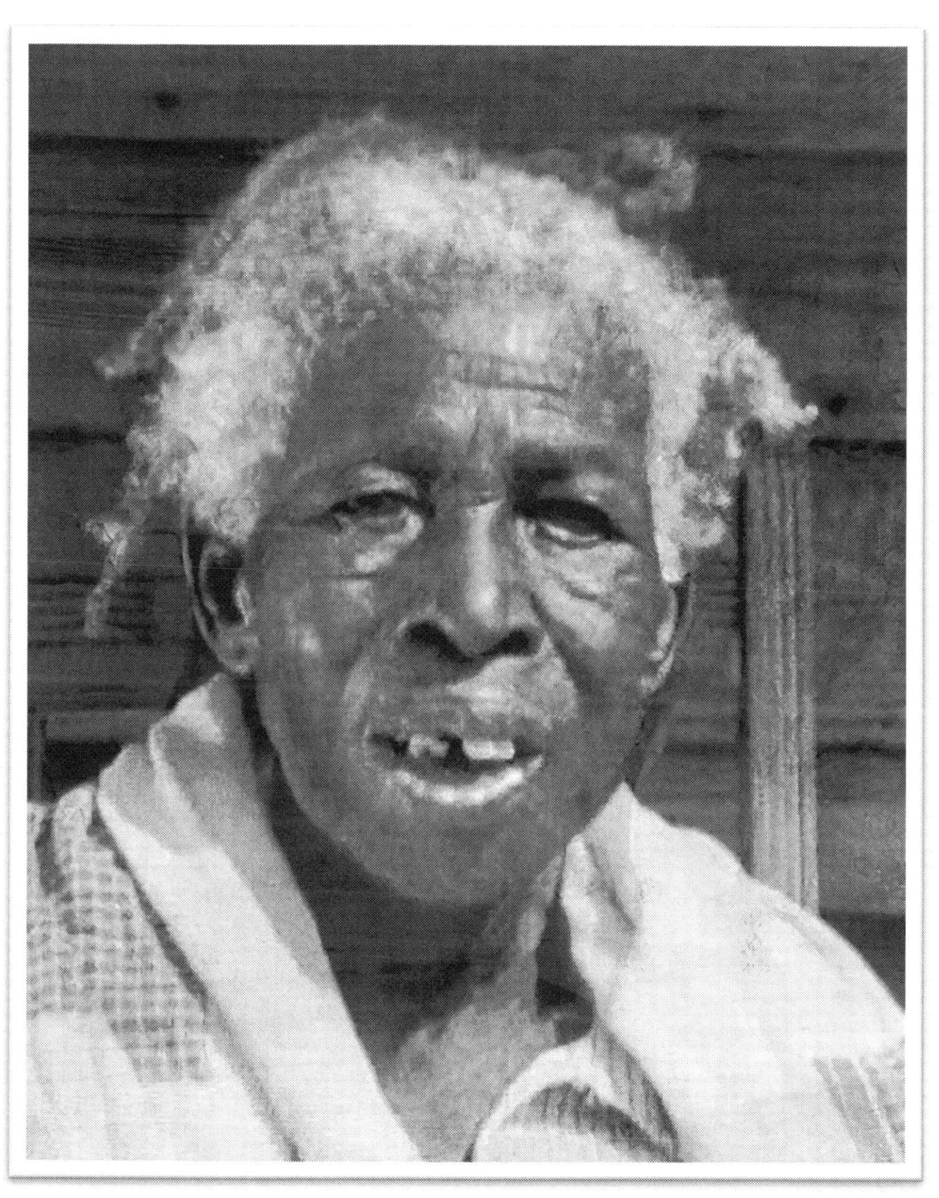

Redoshi was given the name Sally Smith in the U.S. She was mentioned in memoir of Amelia Boynton Robinson who identified her as the last known living survivor of the transatlantic slave trade. She was born around 1848 and lived until 1937. While a slave, she lived on a Bogue Chitto Plantation in Dallas County, having been purchased by Washington Smith, founder of the Bank of Selma and owner of the plantation.

Hannah Durkin, at Newcastle University had previously identified the last surviving slave captured in Africa in the nineteenth century and brought to the United States as Redoshi "Sally" Smith, who died in 1937. But she discovered in 2019 that another former slave, Matilda McCrear, had lived three years later. Matilda died in Selma, Alabama in January 1940 at the age of 83. She would have spoken the West African language of Yoruba. She was said to have worn her hair in a traditional Yoruba style. *(Google Image)*

Amelia Boynton Robinson at the 2015 State of the Union Address: President Barack Obama. Below with President Barack Obama and U.S. Representative Terry Sewell *(Google Image)*

Amelia Boynton Robinson with U.S. Representatives Kevin McCarthy (L), Terry Sewell (C) and John Lewis (R). *(Google Image)*

Amelia Boynton Robinson crossing the Edmund Pettus Bridge with President Obama in March 2015. *(Credit: Doug Mills/TheNew York Times. Google Image)*

(L) Mrs. Boynton Robinson with a fellow marcher in 1965 after being knocked unconscious by Alabama troopers at the bridge. *(Pictorial Parade/Archive Photos/Getty Images)* (R) Joe Jones, who assisted Boynton Robinson in picture on left. *(Google Image)*

Amelia Boynton Robinson February 2014 Guest Speaker at Federal Government Bldg. *(Photo provided by Leon "Chief E. Frazier)*

Lyndon LaRouche, LaRouche Movement-affiliated Schiller Institute with Matriarch of Voting Rights Movement Amelia Boynton Robinson *(Google Image)*

(L-R) Dr. Elaine C Harrington, Atty. Lateefah Muhammad, Amelia Boynton Robinson and Ronnie K. Barnes. *(photo courtesy of Leon E. "Chief" Frazier)*

Amelia Boynton Robinson *(Google Image)*

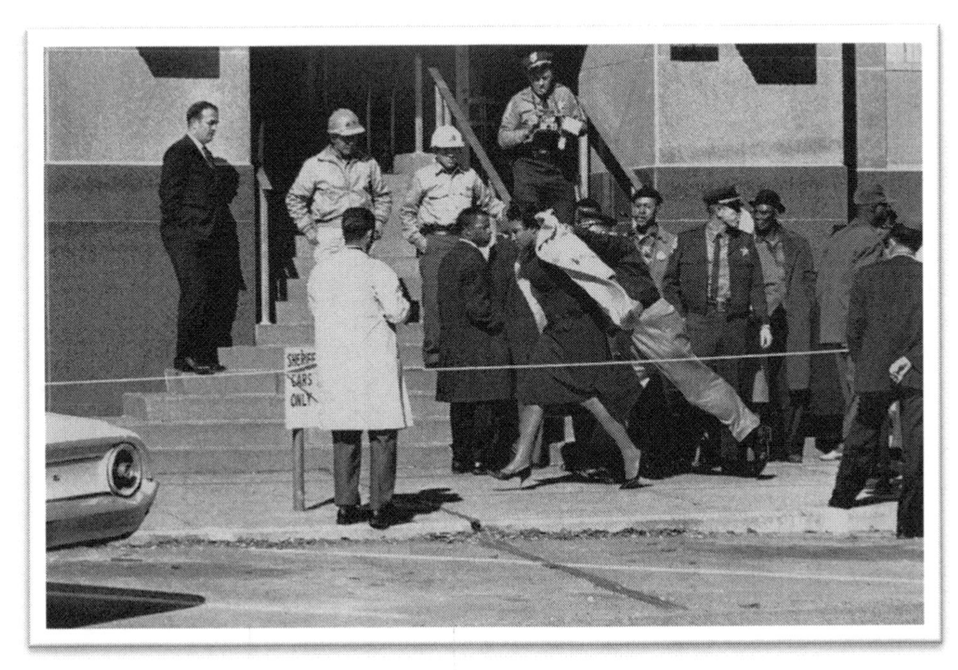

Amelia Boynton Robinson center, is shoved along by the collar by Sheriff Jim Clark while being arrested for seeking to register black voters in Selma, AL Dallas County Courthouse January 19, 1965 *(Horace Cort) (Google Image)*

Chapter 26
Timeline of Events

1905: Amelia Isadora Platts documented date of birth

1911: Amelia Isadora Platts was born in Savannah, Georgia, on August 18, 1911 to George and Anna Eliza (nee Hicks) Platts, both of whom were African American.

1938: Amelia Boynton wrote the stage play, "Through The Years."

1963: After Samuel W Boynton's death, Amelia continued fighting for voting rights and was one of The Courageous Eight, who invited Martin Luther King Jr., and the Southern Christian Leadership Conference to Selma.

1964: In 1964 and 1965 Ms. Boynton worked with Martin Luther King, Diane Nash, James Bevel, and others of the Southern Christian Leadership Conference (SCLC) to plan demonstrations for civil and voting rights.

1964: Boynton Robinson becomes the first black woman to run for the U.S. Congress in Alabama. She garnered 10 percent of the votes at a time when only 2 percent of the voting population was made up of African Americans.

1965: Boynton Robinson was invited to Washington D.C. to see President Lyndon B. Johnson sign the Voting Rights Act on August 6, 1965 giving everyone the right to vote, regardless of their skin color.

1965: Boynton Robinson would become known to many as the "Matriarch of the Voting Rights Movement."

1984: In 1984, she became the co-founding vice president of the Schiller Institute affiliated with Lyndon LaRouche.

1992: Proclamations of "Amelia Boynton Robinson Day" in Seattle and in the state of Washington were rescinded when officials learned of Robinson's involvement in the Schiller Institute.

2007: From September to mid-November 2007, Robinson toured Sweden, Denmark, Germany, France, and Italy in her capacity as vice president of the Schiller Institute.

2013: Franklin Road in Tuskegee, Alabama (Motley Lane to Washington Ave) was renamed "Amelia Boynton Robinson Parkway."

2014: Selma City Council renamed five blocks of Lapsley Street as "Amelia Boynton Robinson and Sam Boynton [Boyntons' Street]."

2015: Boynton Robinson attended President Obama's State of the Union address in January as Congresswoman Terri Sewell's guest of honor.

2015: After suffering a series of strokes, Boynton Robinson died on August 26, 2015 in Montgomery, Alabama eight days after celebrating her 104th birthday.

2016: Representative Terri Sewell (D-Birmingham) proposes a legislature bill to rename Selma's Post Office after Amelia Boynton Robinson. This passed in the U.S. House, awaiting passage in the Senate and the President's signature before the renaming can occur.[91]

---

[91] "Voting Right Act: Timeline." https://www.shmoop.com/historical-texts/votingrights-act/timeline.html.

CHAPTER 27

"The Human Race" - A Poem by Amelia Platts Boynton Robinson

My race is a race of people, Black, White, Yellow and Red,
Colored by all blood and culture, Together we've all been fed.

At first God made himself a man, Placed him in Eden's land of shade,
Gave him control of everything—God's law he obeyed.

Offspring began to move about, East, West, North and South,
Farther & farther from whence he came from the food God had for his mouth.

Man, then began to squabble over God's land, mountain and sea,
Making wars upon his brothers, Wherever he may be.

Man's far from where he used to be. The love he had is gone,
He'll kill his brother's children And will not spare his own.

We put the blame on children. For doing these awful crimes,
Though Mom and Dad had planted hate in their precious little minds.

He starts by saying to the child, "Don't play with him, my dear,"
Immediately the child's mind clicks "Dad, can you be sincere?"

A child of a different color May come to a parent's home,
The child's reminded of Dad's words, Then, his mind begins to roam.

Like a pimple that the thought is planted. "I'm better or greater than they."
That pimple grows a cancer of hate, The thought that is there to stay.

Deeply in his little mind, Thecancerouspimplegrows,
Consumedbyhate he hears each day, Till he feels no respect he owns.

The cancerous hate is now full-blown, He has no respect for you,
His greatest joy is to kill or maim, Matter's not if it's gentile or Jew.

Sisters and brothers, let's search ourselves, Where we've planted that seed of hate.
By telling your kid he's better than they May end up being your fate.

September 5, 1999[92]

[92] Frazier, Leon E. Portraying A Legend In Pictures: The Life & Times of Amelia Platts Boynton Robinson. "Matriarch of the Voting Rights Movements." Tuskegee: L&B Enterprises, 2013.

EPILOGUE

In my home time of Selma, Alabama, beatings and lynchings are what the people had to endure in order for you and I to have the right to vote with full citizenship. At times I was moved to tears as I read and studied all that Amelia Boynton Robinson and other foot soldiers suffered during the Voting Rights Movement.

This city of 28,000 along banks of the Alabama River was deeply segregated. Blacks were forced to drink out of different water fountains, enter restaurants through back doors, and receive medical treatment at specific hospitals—black hospitals to be exact. Although African Americans made up over half of the populations, only about 2% were registered voters.

Boynton Robinson's distinguished efforts in Selma, specifically related to planning and participating in the historic 1965 March from Selma to Montgomery, has earned for her the designated and honorary title: "Matriarch of the Voting Rights Movement."

Amelia Boynton Robinson, a prominent activist for voting rights, was beaten unconscious for her efforts. A photo of her sprawled out in the street became the iconic picture that immortalized the march now known as "Bloody Sunday." The graphic footage shocked the nation and moved President Johnson to release a statement protesting the brutality of the police running rampant over the defenseless protesters. Pictures were shown across the nation on national television of lawmen smashing billy clubs across the heads of marchers stampeding by foot and on horseback as they ran over the demonstrators. Many were injured and bruised with the scars and trauma from that day lasting for the rest of their lives.

While writing this manuscript, I have to admit that feelings of anxiety, depression, and even posttraumatic stress periodically dashed in and out of my mind as came to understand the acts of blatant racism and bigotry in the South under Jim Crow that ruled the land. However, it helped me through some of my trying times that I've experienced with my health and dealing with some family members' mental illness that we've been going through this past year.

Even now as I think about the COVID-19 epidemic that has swept across the world, this, too, brings on a lot of anxiety, depression and posttraumatic stress for me and others. But it has also given me comfort and therapy being under quarantine for two months has allowed me to relax my mind off the crisis America faces and finish this book.

So, as I read about Marie foster and Annie Cooper and other unsung heroes of the Movement, I reminisce briefly of being in the company of them both once upon a time. Concerning Marie, I thought back to the early 1980s when Faye Ora Rose Touré (aka, Rose Sanders) introduced her at one of the annual bridge crossing marches [in its infancy at that time]. Faye Ora Rose announced to the small crowd gathered that she was one of the original foot soldiers from the 1960s who had marched and was beaten on the Edmund Pettus Bridge on "Bloody Sunday."

Marie had been at the front of the march behind Boynton Robinson in Selma on "Bloody Sunday." She turned around waving her hands and smiled with pride that she was once again getting ready to march, representing all those who had fought, bled and died for me to be there with her that day.

Marie even had on the same shoes on that she had worn on that "Bloody Sunday." She then smiled and took off one of the shoes off and waived it in the air so we all could see it. That was an inspiring moment for me, as I was only about 15 years old at the time.

Concerning Annie Cooper, I met her at a next-door neighbor's house one summer when I was about the age of 12. I was there with my younger brother Tyrone, sitting on the sofa waiting for my neighbor Ms. Ruth Barnes (no relation to me), to get ready so we could leave in Annie's 1960s Cadillac. When she finally came out, she asked my brother and me if we knew who this was. We both said that we didn't, so Annie looked at us and told Ruth that we were too young to know about the civil rights movement and "Bloody Sunday."

My godmother Ruth looked at me and my brother in dismay and said, "Well you better get to know who she is and remember that name Annie Cooper. She's the one who beat up that Sheriff Clark at that courthouse when he grabbed her while she was standing in line at the Dallas County Courthouse protesting for the right to vote. Annie knocked him off his feet and there was nothing he could do but call for help from the other deputies. Annie shook her head and looked dismayed that Mrs. Barnes kept talking about it. Needlessly to say, Ms. Barnes was right: I do remember and can share it with you. It was just like Ruth had said: Annie Cooper has gone down in history.

I have carefully read Amelia's *Bridge Across Jordan* memoir in order to understand the message she was giving the world. She and her husband Samuel William "Bill" Boynton felt and showed compassion for the people of Selma and Dallas County. As graduates of Tuskegee Institute in the 1920s, upon their arrival to Selma, Bill and Amelia saw that the poor, disenfranchised Blacks in Selma and Dallas County needed help in seeing that they were just one step above slavery with no future in farming as sharecroppers.

For sure, the Boyntons knew that the black people in Selma were emancipated, however, the problem was the Blacks in Selma didn't realize they needed help because most didn't see that as sharecroppers they were living just this one step above enslavement. And some Blacks in Dallas County and Selma were even living like indentured servants—being promised something that the plantation owners and white landlord overseers knew they weren't going to get, namely, their own land and property or freedom.

Oh yes! It was promised to some: "If you and your family maintain the cotton fields and the crops based on production and surplus you will be able to purchase your own land and the property would be yours." But it never happened. Some blacks ended up staying on Mr. John's land until the voting right act was passed and progression toward true emancipation started thereafter.

Amelia's son Bruce Boynton summarizes it up best. Bruce explained to me that to some his mother is considered to be the "Mother of the Voting Rights Act." "I was fortunate to be born to parents who were dedicated to black people gaining their civil rights and acquiring property instead of living on the white landlords' property as a sharecropper." He added, "My mother lived until she was 103 and during her entire life, she was devoted to being involved in things that would advance her race." (As noted in record books, documents as well as what Amelia Boynton Robinson had said before her passing, put her age as around 110.) Bruce also expressed to me that what's mentioned in this book, while true, it represents only a small portion of what she contributed to the world.

The movement started in Selma, Alabama, long before Dr. King arrived on the scene. As the late Rev. James L. Bevel stated following the 1995 performance in Washington D.C. of the play, "Through The Years" written by Boynton Robinson in 1936, "Before the world knew that there was a Martin Luther King, Jr., C.T. Vivian, Andrew Young, or Hosea Williams, or before Bernard Lafayette, James Bevel, John Lewis, Marion Barry or Diane Nash were born, Amelia and her husband Bill were fighting for literacy and voting rights in Selma for African American people with love."[93]

Bill and Amelia Boynton soon became known as "Mr. and Mrs. Civil Rights" around Selma after Whites started noticing the couple teaching Blacks how to buy their own farming land and homes, and enlightening them on how to register and vote. The Boyntons were soon told by local white officials that they couldn't be teaching blacks how to vote, or how to manage their finances.

With threats and rage, Whites tried to run the Boyntons out of town. However, this didn't stop them. They continued and initiated the revitalization of the Dallas County Voting Rights League in the early 1930s. The Boyntons had many opportunities to leave Selma, but they chose to stay and fight for freedom, justice, and voting rights for black

---

[93] Amelia Boynton Robinson. "About the Matriarch of the Voters Rights Movement & Her Family." http://www.ameliaboyntonrobinson.org/about.html. Pagel.htm.

people who felt inferior to their white counterparts.

Established Jim Crow laws impacted literacy tests and poll taxes which were instituted to disenfranchise African Americans and keep them from voting.

Amelia became the first woman in America to serve as a county agent with the United States Department of Agriculture. The Boyntons were the first Blacks in Alabama to own an insurance company, as well as a real estate and employment agency. Together, she and Bill helped to raise funds that built a community center in Selma that was used primarily by African Americans. Prior to that, Blacks had no facility where they could hold events as the white citizens of Selma did—and that building still stands to this day.

The Boyntons raised the moral and intellectual standards of black people through education. In 1936, Amelia wrote the play "Through The Years" to further inspire Blacks and to raise funds to carry on the liberation struggle.

The Matriarch of the Civil Rights Movement, was also responsible for the national school lunch program that started after a 1967 visit to a Selma elementary school by then Assistant to the USDA Secretary, William M. Seabron. He acted upon Amelia's request for such a program.

Under a model established by the Boyntons in Dallas county, hundreds of acres of land were purchased between the 1940s and 1960s to help poor Blacks end sharecropping for others and to begin producing crops for themselves.

Despite the reality of white retaliation, African American residents continued to call for civil rights. In 1955, Bill and Amelia Boynton testified before a Senate subcommittee in Washington, D.C. regarding African American suffrage. Their testimony contributed to the passage of the Civil Rights Act of 1957.

In the 1960s, the Boyntons found their business at 21 Franklin Street under economic attack because it was recognized as the meeting place for the Dallas County Voters League and other civil rights local groups in the area like the SCLC and SNCC.

Amelia was a cofounder of the Voting Rights Institute and Museum, as well as the Annual Jubilee that commemorates "Bloody Sunday" in Selma.

The recipient of numerous awards and citations, Amelia Boynton Robinson was awarded the Martin Luther King Jr. Freedom Medal in 1990. In 2005, during the commemoration of the "Bloody Sunday" March, SCLC/W.O.M.E.N., Incorporated of Atlanta and the National Voting Rights Institute and Museum of Selma unveiled a monument in Mrs. Robinson's honor at the foot of the Edmund Pettus Bridge.

In 2007, the Southern Christian Leadership Conference honored her with its highest award, the Rosa Parks Award, in their celebration. That award had been established in 1962 by Dr. King when he served as president of the organization. Amelia was a member of the Daughters of Isis, Miriam Court #110, and an honorary member of the Delta Sigma Theta Sorority.

Amelia was bestowed an Honorary Doctorate at the National Conference of Black Lawyers by Community College of Law and International Diplomacy in Chicago in May 1996.

She was married to Samuel W. Boynton in 1936 and their marriage lasted for 27 years until his untimely death on May 13, 1963.

Besides their sons Bruce and Samuel William "Bill" Boynton II, Amelia helped to raise her youngest brother George's daughters, Germaine Platts Bowser and Sharon Platts Seay as her own daughters.

Amelia's son, Bruce Boynton, is now a retired attorney. He made news during the civil rights era in 1958 when he was arrested at a segregated bus stop waiting room in Virginia. He was seated at a whites-only lunch counter on his way home to Selma from Howard University in Washington, D.C. He appealed his arrest and conviction to the U.S. Supreme Court, which resulted in a federal order desegregating interstate travel facilities. His historic case, Boynton vs Virginia, won by Thurgood Marshall in the U.S. Supreme Court decision in 1960, ultimately produced the Freedom Riders from its verdict. And it would be the last case argued by Thurgood Marshall before he became United States Solicitor General, eventually becoming the first black Supreme Court Justice.

In 2011, Amelia's family established the Amelia Boynton Robinson Foundation. Amelia's son Bruce and his wife Betty Strong Boynton sponsored this nonprofit organization, which can be found on her social media page.

In addition, the house which she and her husband Bill called home in Selma was added to the Alabama Register by the Alabama Historical Commission in 2008. Their house was also placed on the list of Places in Peril by the Commission, which allows funding to be secured to help with its restoration.

Amelia had high hopes of the house being named a National Historic Site someday, since so many civil and voting right icons and others visited it over the years. These included dignitaries and renowned individuals such George Washington Carver, Dr. Martin Luther King Jr., Mary McLeod Bethune, Ralph Buch, Robert Kennedy, Duke Ellington, Dorothy Height, Joan Baez, Count Basie, John Lewis, James Bevel, Joseph Lowery Jr, Andrew Young, and many others.

In 2013 a portion of Franklin Road, extending from Motley Lane to Washington Avenue in Tuskegee Alabama, was renamed "Amelia Boynton Robinson Parkway."

Lawmakers have the power today to stamp out racial discrimination, to create racial "equality as a fact" (to quote LBJ) if they want to.[94] They have a chance to embrace the antiracist cause of genuine equality, remembering what protestors chanted back in the 1960s as they called for freedom as promised by the Emancipation Proclamation. Unfortunately, local and federal lawmakers fear repercussions from campaign donors and voters. They know that post racialists would protest antiracism bills as discriminatory and representing hate toward white people just as slavers and segregationists did before them—even if the bill would benefit most Americans including white people.

As seen in the twenty-first century, those who have the power to completely abolish racial discrimination have not done so as of yet. It is reasonable to think that they will never be persuaded or educated to do so

---

[94] Kendi, 508.

as long as racism benefits them in some way.

There have been those in power who have attempted to abolish racial disparities through their influence and diversity training. However, these continue to be the exception rather than the rule. Others could argue also that generations of racist ideas have been educated and persuaded to be conclusions in their thinking of race ideology. To say the least, it has been proven Americans have let go of old racists ideas. Somewhat. However, new racist ideas have continuously been manifested to remind Americans that racism isn't over.

The Voting Rights Movement started in Selma with local protests of discriminatory practices regarding the right to vote as African Americans. The Selma Movement expanded to become statewide protests for voting rights, and state-wide protests became national protests and national protest became international protests.

For Selma it started with Amelia and Samuel W. Boynton. And their jobs as county agents for the United States Federal Agriculture Department allowed them to mobilize sharecroppers and others to gain the right to vote and have ownership of farmland, as well homeownership coupled with financial literacy.

Amelia Boynton Robinson, the Matriarch of the Civil Rights Movement, ultimately gave America the Voting Rights Act. It was her love for humanity that gave her the courage to fight for an equitable society that gave to all the right to vote with full citizenship.

Today, Alabama's iconic civil rights town of Selma is now the fastest shrinking city in the state. Deteriorated, abandoned storefronts and warehouses are in view of the riverfront on Water Avenue near the St. James Hotel and the Edmund Pettus Bridge. There are plenty of For Sale signs in a lot of the buildings that pre-date the Civil War in downtown Selma. Today, the Selma population shows signs of disenfranchisement, both economically and politically. Some could make a case that it makes Selma, the symbol of past civil rights victories, is a symbol of current civil rights failures.

ACKNOWLEDGMENTS

I would like to acknowledge all the people I know and do not know who assisted and supported me in composing *Amelia Boynton Robinson: Matriarch of the Voting Rights Movement*. And to my ever-supportive family members and friends, to all the unsung thinkers, dead and alive, whose works on civil rights, voting rights and race have helped shape my thinking and this history—I thank you. No doubt, this book is as much by you as it is by me.

I initially had no plans to write this book. I intended to write on a fascinating subject of interest—something about the fact that we are spiritual beings having a human experience. But I felt the calling of my spiritual ancestors beckoning me to tell an untold side of a story of someone I'm calling a modern-day Harriet Tubman, Amelia Boynton Robinson.

I would like to acknowledge my journalism instructor, at the University of Alabama in Tuscaloosa, Marie Parsons, who first saw my writing ability and pushed me to continue to where I am today. I also want to acknowledge Carol Howell, my writing instructor at the University of Alabama who mentored me until she felt I was ready to sail on my own. And to my most recent journalism workshop instructor, author Linda Alexander, I would like to express much appreciation for making me comfortable and exposing me to the thought of writing biographies. I had no thoughts of wanting to do so until you taught me that it's okay to think outside of the box and pursue other genres in the world of nonfiction writing.

I would also like to thank one of my mentors, North Eastern Regional Area Director Linda M. White who gave me the opportunity to work and serve in several capacities for the federal government. Linda also became the 26th International President of Alpha Kappa Alpha (AKA) Sorority. Acknowledgement also goes out to Nancy G. Sewell Librarian Media Specialist extraordinaire and the first African American city councilwoman in Selma, Alabama. Thank you, Nancy, for your mentorship and encouragement to continue on my journey in life. Nancy's former positions with the AKA sorority have included as International Secretary, and South Eastern Regional Director.

This book has added light and enabled me to understand and appreciate the Voting and Civil Right Movements more than I could ever imagine as I learned of the obstacles African Americans had to endure including enslavement, emancipation, sharecropping and Jim Crow. It gives me hope that there are people in the world who still believe in humanity who do not engage in discriminatory practices against others because of race, creed, color or gender.

I would like to give a special acknowledgement to my parents, Mary Laura and Cleveland Barnes, as well as to my brothers, Tyrone and Willie and my sister Annie Mae Barnes Heard. Love is truly a verb, and I thank you for your love.

A special note of thanks goes to my sister-in-law Myrline Tyus Barnes and a thank you to everyone else who played any part in the completion of this manuscript.

Amelia Boynton Robinson also had a special team of caregivers based out of Tuskegee, Alabama who looked out for her in all the endeavors she pursued up until her retirement from this earth. They were Leon E. "Chief" Frazier, Lateefah Muhammad, and Harriet P. Oliver.

I am also much appreciative of Shawn Eckles for giving me some direction in communication with the Boynton family. Shawn has worked with the Amelia Boynton Robinson Foundation in helping to market the Boyntons' brand by reaching out and connecting with people about the life and legacy of Amelia Boynton Robinson.

ABOUT THE AUTHOR

A resident of Montgomery, Alabama, Ronnie Kennedy Barnes holds a Master of Science degree in Human Resource Management from Troy State University (Montgomery, Alabama campus). He completed a number of graduate courses in business writing and management communication at David N. Myers University in Cleveland, Ohio.

Ronnie also holds a Bachelor of Arts degree in Communication from the University of Alabama, with a major in public relations and a double minor in business management and military science. His mass communication courses included a concentration in print journalism. Barnes was a freelance writer for the university's student newspaper, *The Crimson White*. In addition, Barnes received his commission from the University of Alabama ROTC department into the Adjutant General Officer Corps.

Upon completion of his undergraduate degree, he became a scholarship recipient to attend the University of South Carolina Southeastern Multicultural Newspaper Workshop for a semester where he received a broad range of training in print journalism. He wrote and edited feature stories for *The New Reporter* newspaper as part of the graduation requirements.

After graduating, Barnes interned as a freelance reporter at the *Selma Times Journal*. He completed a second internship in print journalism with *The Plain Dealer* newspaper in Cleveland, Ohio where he was a copy boy and shadow reporter. Barnes continued to work at various newspapers and magazines as a freelance writer for the next six years in Cleveland.

Ronnie Barnes also holds an Associate of Science degree from George Wallace State College in Selma, Alabama and an Associate of Arts degree from the University of Maryland in College Park, Maryland (European Division Headquarters).

Barnes is the author of the book *The New Joyful Sounds.* He has also published numerous personal journals for purchase on Amazon.com. And he has also created various products like popsockets and designer T-shirts, also available on Amazon.com.

Barnes is a U.S. Army veteran and a former government employee who retired after 25 years of service.

Made in the USA
Columbia, SC
08 June 2023

17731414R00124